I0139456

The Awareness Game

An Easy, Four Step Approach for Changing, Improving, and Creating the Life You Want

Where Did You Play Today?

Pete Wanger and Jane Wanger Falke

THOMAS NOBLE BOOKS

Wilmington, DE

THOMAS NOBLE
BOOKS

Copyright © 2020 Jane Wanger Falke. All rights reserved. No portion of this book may be reproduced mechanically, electronically, or by any other means, including photocopying, without written permission from the author. It is illegal to copy this book, post it to a website, or distribute it by any other means without permission from the author.

The phrase, The Awareness Game™, was originally copyrighted on October 11, 1991 by Peter K. Wanger and Jane C. M. Wanger. This book is an updated and revised version of that work.

Thomas Noble Books
Wilmington, DE

ISBN: 978-1-945586-28-6

First Printing: 2020

This publication is designed to provide accurate and authoritative information regarding the subject matter covered. It is sold with the understanding that the author is not engaged in rendering professional services. If legal, accounting, medical, psychological, or any other expert assistance is required, the services of a competent professional person should be sought.

Praise for The Awareness Game

JoAnne's Story - How *The Awareness Game* changed my life

I met Pete when I was 25 years old and I was hired on as his gardener. He shared The Awareness Game *with me early on. At that age, I was just learning my way in the world, often stumbling on interpersonal relationships and struggling to find my path. However, with the tools from 'The Game Plan', I was able to run my landscaping business and start a successful home management service. Instead of wasting time on "False Agreements", "Disagreements", or "Separation", I learned to ask myself: "What is working?", "What isn't working?", and "What could work better?". I learned to avoid unrealistic or false expectations and take responsibility for my actions and my successes.*

I was fortunate to start using 'The Game Plan' so early in life. I built on my learning experiences throughout the years that followed, advancing through my career to become a horticulture educator and then an associate professor with the University of Nevada, Reno. When I was promoted into leadership roles, and was in charge of staff, I used what I'd learned from The Awareness Game *to coach them, to evaluate their performances, and to guide them toward greater growth and success. I used the principles of 'The Game Plan' to enhance my collaborations with colleagues across the country, providing educational materials that improved people's lives.*

I continue to use the principles: "Be clear, be fair, be truthful, and be responsible". Thanks to The Awareness Game, *I found a path that was not only successful, but joyful.*

—JoAnne Skelly, associate professor and extension educator emerita

Meri's Story - How *The Awareness Game* helped my life

The Awareness Game *came into my life at a time when I was a member of four elected or appointed community boards. My earnest desire was to serve my community and the democratic process.* The Awareness Game *gave me the tools to do so by guiding me in how to be clear, fair, truthful, and responsible.* The Game *showed me how to focus on achieving attainable goals, how to communicate well with others, how to understand my personal commitments, and how to evaluate my role in success.*

The beautiful artwork on The Chart conveyed each condition in my life graphically, and as a dynamic, aspirational journey. The Chart provided years of illuminating discussion with friends, family, and colleagues; and The Awareness Game *continues to inform my life.*

—Meri McEneny, business owner, community volunteer, meditator

Acknowledgments

I am deeply grateful to all the people who supported the development of *The Awareness Game* over the past years: Cathy McClelland who sat tirelessly while Pete described the path and each of the characters on The Chart so she could draw a visual aid for understanding; JoAnne for the continued typewritten changes that helped to improve *The Game*; Michael who was always there to listen, offer ideas and video Pete's workshop; Steve for his friendship and marketing ideas; Eric for ideas and skills on offering 'The Awareness Game' as a workshop; Meri for her encouragement and support; Dave who made recent changes on The Chart and the illustrations in the book; Robin for her writing style on my biography; Lynne who supported me through the writing and publishing process; and my friends and family who encouraged me to complete this unique and wonderful project to help others make a better life for themselves. Most of all, Pete who wouldn't give up on me and helped me to grow. Thank you.

CONTENTS

A Message from Pete

Dear players,

The ideas and concepts expressed in *The Awareness Game* have been developed over a period of many years. My brother, Merv, and I had a very successful business in the San Francisco area. Our successes came from the excitement of creating and selling new products, from providing the best quality at the best prices, and from doing our jobs together in alignment, creating profit-making products.

We only had one rule. No new project was approved without the agreement of the five top executives. When you wanted to do something— or change something— you had to get the approval of the other four. Agreement was the key to our success.

The Awareness Game is based on that sentiment—agreement on your ideas, agreement from those involved, and then, agreement to do something and doing it. *The Awareness Game* will teach you a method that will make your life easier and effortless.

Although many of the stories are from my personal experience, *The Awareness Game* is a co-creation of the hundreds of people who have contributed to the material by sharing their experiences with me.

The help, the insights, the doubts, the encouragement, and the time and love of so many people have made *The Awareness Game* possible. My deepest appreciation goes out to all of you for your contribution.

Enjoy *The Awareness Game*. It is the answer to all your problems and a method for a successful life.

Sincerely,

Pete Wanger
Incline Village, Nevada

Jane's Introduction

I met Pete Wanger in 1979. Pete was one of the owners and teachers at a business school I attended. The Burklyn Business School was a six-week live-in experience. The school offered business subjects using accelerated learning techniques that taught people how to develop their own businesses and become entrepreneurs. They also provided a holistic approach to wellbeing, with exercise, body work, meditation, and diet awareness.

Pete was developing a method to bring more consciousness and awareness into people's lives, relationships, and businesses. This method was born during my Burklyn experience. It was called *The Awareness Game*.

It began when Pete retired from a successful snack food business at the age of 48. Pete and his brother bought a defunct potato chip company that they then turned into a success. They developed a successful management style that promoted fairness and integrity. They worked for 20 years to build the business and make the company successful, and then sold the company and retired.

One day, Pete was encouraged by family and friends to take a course that changed his life. It was a course that taught him that he was responsible for creating what was in his life: all the good, bad, sad, unpleasant and pleasurable things that happened to him.

But he was confused. How could he be responsible for the times when someone had hurt him? He did understand how he created successes in his life through his desires and efforts, but the unhappy times just *happened* to him. If he really was responsible for the good and the bad that happened to him, how could he create more of what he wanted and less of what he didn't want?

He began to reflect on his life and ask more questions. How did he and his brother create a successful business? Why was it that life was so good to him most of the time? Was he just lucky? How did he contribute to making his life the way it was? As Pete observed the life that was around him, in other people, and in the world, answers came to him. The method he had used to make his snack food company successful helped make his life better, providing him with more awareness and more success. After years of testing this method, *The Awareness Game* was born.

Pete and I married in 1981. Our relationship was built on the methods and principles that we were developing for *The Awareness Game*. It was not easy to expose my whole life during our marriage. Pete and I both had a lot of past emotional traumas to clear up before we were operating in a positive flow with our individual life and with each other. As we used *The Awareness Game*, over time, our life together and personal growth began to flow with more balance and support. *The Awareness Game* evolved into a tool that provided us with more success and strengthened our confidence as individuals.

In 1991, Pete was diagnosed with cancer. Six months later, he passed away. His only regret was that he didn't spread *The Awareness Game* to the world for the benefit of others. The night we said our goodbyes, I heard myself saying to him, "I'll get *The Awareness Game* out to the world for you." I was surprised by what I'd said. This project was Pete's dream. I was just his supporter in the development.

Fast forward to 2019. My Lake Tahoe friends inspired me to write a book about *The Awareness Game* and to get it out into the world so that others could create a better, more conscious life for themselves. I thought about it, then recalled my last words to Pete: "I'll get *The Awareness Game* out to the world for you." I pulled out the manuals and The Chart on The Game. After reviewing them, I felt ready to share our work with you. Much of the information and the stories throughout this guidebook were inspired by Pete. However, I felt I had to put my own twist on this important work. So, *The Awareness Game* is a co-created effort.

Play *The Awareness Game*. It will give you an understanding of why your life is what it is and will change the negative influences and unsatisfactory outcomes you may be experiencing. I promise you it will change your life for the better, just as it has for so many others.

Sincerely,

Jane Wanger Falke
Carlsbad, California

What's It All About?

What if you could have a life with mostly positive outcomes? What if you could experience your life the way you want it to be and gain confidence in yourself, support from others, satisfaction with your life, and security about your future? Would you want it?

Of course you would. That's what *The Awareness Game* is all about.

Even though each of us is a unique individual and all want different things in our lives, there are life experiences everyone shares. We want to experience **Wellbeing** and a **Balanced** life with **Success** rather than disappointment or failure, **Support** rather than resistance or disapproval, **Satisfaction** rather than resentment or feelings of rejection, and **Security** rather than uncertainty or fear of the future.

Success in your life builds inner strength, confidence, and clarity. Support from others provides motivation and cooperation. Satisfaction in what you are doing strengthens good feelings and happiness. Security adds more certainty about your future pursuits. This is a balanced life. *The Awareness Game* has a simple method to show you how to have this balanced life and the wellbeing that goes along with it.

I recently watched a concert film, *Happiness Continues,* put on by the Jonas Brothers. They shared their personal story about the experience of the group breaking up and then reforming. Nick said, "The journey we all went on was a way to find our inner child and reconnect with who we are inside." The three brothers love playing music together. This desire drove them back together.

Sure, they had to work on themselves and being supportive of each other. Nick said, "We hashed it out and talked it through." This is what it is like to Cross the Bridge of Courage on *The Awareness Game* Chart. Whether they had help in understanding each other, or worked on their issues alone, they had unknowingly followed the principles of *The Awareness Game*. They can now continue their Success in the music they share; Support in their relationship; Satisfaction in offering their talents to the world, doing what they love together; and Security in their future by giving to the world their positive musical message. This struggle and comeback is an example of what can be. *The Awareness Game* is a method for changing, improving, and creating what can be.

Have you found your path? Many people are not creating the life they want. They're self-conscious, lack confidence, don't know where to go or what to do, or they feel that they are better than others and use critical and demanding behavior. When you think these thoughts and have these feelings about yourself or others, you develop beliefs and behaviors that become habits of thinking, feeling, and acting. You no longer have awareness or conscious control of these beliefs and behaviors. You remain stuck in your life with little movement, or you may even feel you are stuck in a downward spiral.

The Awareness Game helps you to identify beliefs and behaviors that are standing in your way when you are on the path shown on the left side of *The Chart*: "Unaware of the What Works". When you recognize these obstacles, you can change your course of action by using the solutions along the path that will move you to the right side of *The Chart*: "Playing at What Works."

The Awareness Game is about helping people out of unpleasant, uncomfortable and unsatisfactory feelings and situations. If this is your life now, *The Awareness Game* will help you change direction and move into the areas of your life that bring you more satisfaction and happiness. It's time to wake up, be more aware of who you are, and take control of what's going on in your life. Help is on the way!

Whether you want to improve through education or grow personally, be a competent worker or a loving spouse and parent, or develop a skill, a business or product, *The Awareness Game* can work for you. The more you use the principles of *The Awareness Game*, the sooner these principles will form new habits and behaviors, and soon you will be playing *The Awareness Game* naturally and successfully every day with positive outcomes.

Many of us encourage our children, friends and family to develop, find and follow their paths and interests, and you should be doing the same for yourself. Take some time to care for yourself and reflect on your day. Ask yourself, "Is my day going as I planned? Is my current life what I want? If things were going well in my life, what would that be like?"

Right now, think about a few areas of your life that you would like to change, improve and create. Write them down below. Later in this guidebook, you will define these areas with more clarity and detail. Then, you will begin to use *The Game Plan* process for achieving success.

I want to change, improve and create these in my life:

Success - Control over my life

Example: To know what I want; to have more self-confidence; to be better at something

_____   _____

_____   _____

Support - Relationships with others

Example: To be more compassionate; to get along better with others; to communicate better

_____   _____

_____   _____

Satisfaction - Overall contentment and fulfillment in my life

Example: Better health; enjoy what I'm doing; experience more happiness

_____   _____

_____   _____

Security - Sense of certainty about my future

Example: Financial abundance; comfortable living environment; overcome uncertainty about something

_____   _____

_____   _____

You can't help others unless you help yourself first. Learn and grow. Become more conscious, a better person, and express the best of you each day along the way. You are here to learn from your experiences and personally grow. Work on yourself like you would hone a new skill. Your life on Earth is an investment in yourself. Make it how you want it to be while you are on this planet. Be an example to others.

The top right side of *The Chart*, "What Works", is where you want to be all the time. By using the four principles of *The Game Plan* you will learn a new way of managing your life with more successful outcomes.

Here's How It Works

The Awareness Game uses this guidebook and a Chart, shown on the cover. The guidebook gives you an understanding of The Game and teaches you how to identify what is causing your unsatisfactory results and how to improve your outcomes. It offers a method that will help you, rather than outside forces, to be the director of your life, Playing at What Works.

The Chart is a road map that shows you where you are, how you got there, and what you can do to get to where you want to be. We will go over each part of The Chart in more detail as you read this guidebook.

The Chart consists of three parts:

1) **Unaware of What Works** - This is where you are continually having unsuccessful experiences. Eventually, the path gets more uncomfortable and stressful. Unaware of What Works is a cycle of Conditioned Behavior where you keep repeating unsatisfactory experiences. But there is a way out!

2) **Discovering What Works** - Discovering What Works has two parts:

Part 1 - *Climbing Out of The Pits*. You have two choices here. You can ignore the discomfort of The Pits and go back and live your life on the path of Conditioned Behavior with other people, or you can use The Keys To Awareness, to move you to the Bridge of Courage and then up the path to Playing at What Works.

Part 2 - *Moving Through Pit Stop #2*. This is where you think you are doing all the right things, but not everything is working out as you'd planned. Even though it may be a little uncomfortable, know that you are evolving and that Pit Stop #2 is a higher level of awareness. You know you are involved in an unsatisfactory experience but don't understand how you got to Pit Stop #2. You can use The Formula to move out of Pit Stop #2 to the Bridge of Courage and then up the path to Playing at What Works.

3) **Playing at What Works** - Playing at What Works has two parts:

Part 1 - *Crossing the Bridge of Courage*. You have used the solutions along the path, whether in The Pits, or by having a stopover in Pit Stop #2. It's time to clear up the past and use The Three-step Method; and move on to What Works, using The Game Plan to make changes, improve something, and create your life to be the best it can be.

Part 2 - *What Works*. This is where you are designing how you want your life to be and are achieving better and better outcomes using the principles of The Game Plan.

It's important to understand that everyone plays at all levels of The Chart at one time or another. Even the most successful people have unsatisfactory experiences. But unsatisfactory experiences help you grow, learn more about yourself, and understand what you truly want. By looking at The Chart, you can identify unsatisfactory experiences, see the path ahead, and then use the available solutions to improve or change what you don't want into What Works for you.

Only you can fulfill your needs and wants. No one else can do it for you, so make your life happen. Create it the way you want it to be. Experience wellbeing and a balanced life with more successful outcomes, support from others, personal satisfaction, and certainty about your future. It's all available here. The Awareness Game works! All you have to do to make it happen is apply the principles of The Game Plan, and the solutions when needed, to your life.

Now, let's move on. You are about to learn and understand each part of The Chart. We begin at Unaware of What Works—the left side of The Chart. This will demonstrate how we cause the unfavorable experiences in our life, and how to get out of the cycle of Conditioned Behavior.

Part I

UNAWARE OF WHAT WORKS
Conditioned Behavior

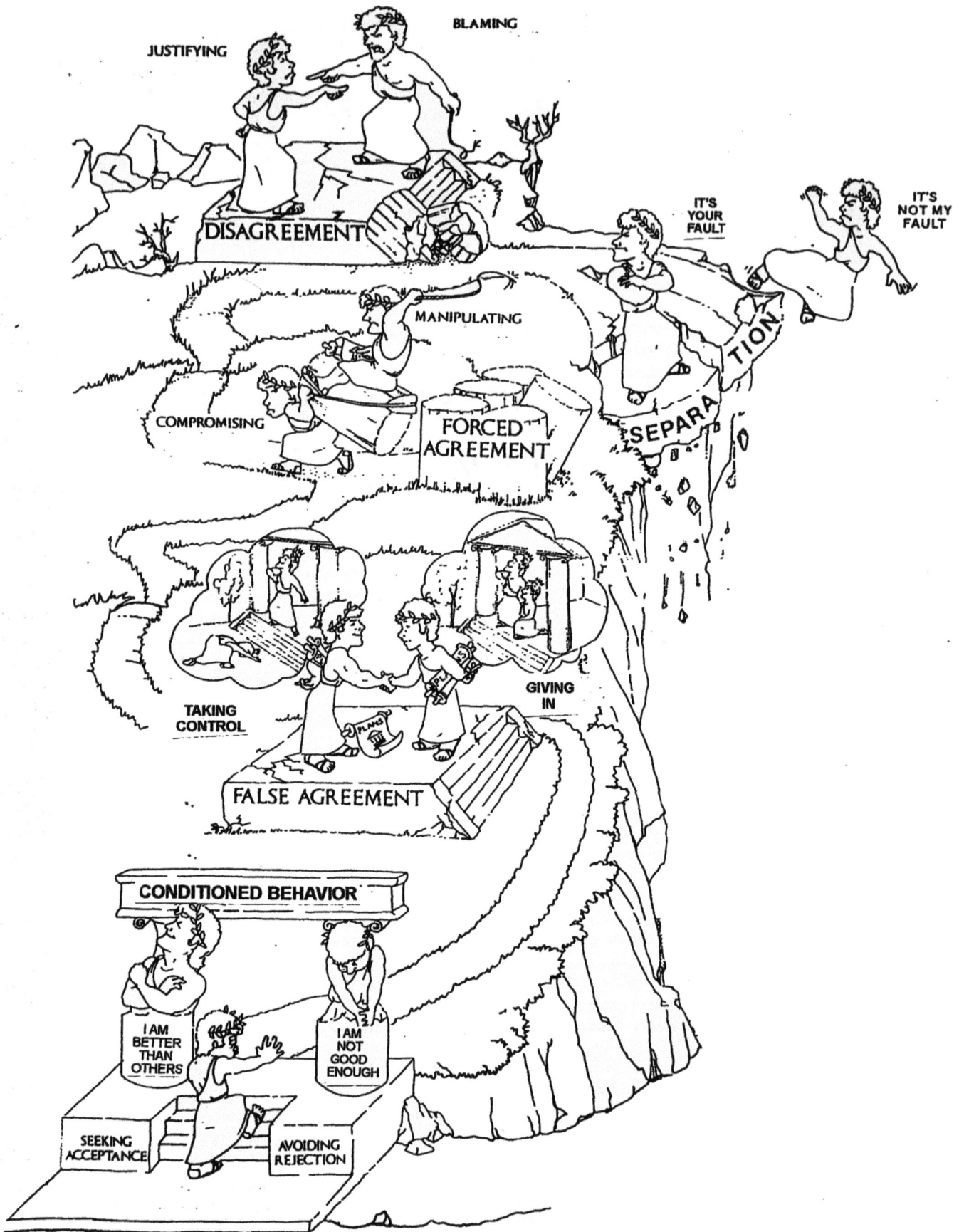

UNAWARE OF WHAT WORKS

Have you ever felt like your life isn't turning out the way you had hoped? Or felt you were a victim of circumstances and there was nothing you could do about it?

Sometimes life gives us unsatisfactory experiences. People hurt our feelings. We get angry. We are bored or depressed. We feel forced or pressured to act a certain way or to do something we don't want to do. Our lives seem to be moving in a vicious cycle where unsatisfactory experiences, results, or outcomes keep happening over and over.

From Ano Ano The Seed, by Kristin Zambucka.
(early Hawaiian culture)
And they were taught the laws of life... that their treatment
of others would return at last upon themselves.
Those who cheat will be cheated.
Those who slander will be slandered.
For every lie you tell... you will be lied to.
Brutality will meet with brutality.
We get what we give and to the same degree.
And not always from the same people with whom we've dealt.
But somewhere... sometime... someone will treat you in like manner.
The good that we do to others will return also.
For your kindness to strangers, you will receive hospitality in far places yourself.
Understand the troubles of others who come to you with their souls bared...
and when you cry yourself, you will be sympathetically understood.
We get what we give. Like always attracts like.
This is the law and it is inevitable.
We cannot escape the results of our actions.

There are reasons for this.

When we are born on planet Earth, we become subject to its forces. Gravity is the force that keeps our bodies anchored to Earth. When you throw a ball up in the air, it will fall to the ground. It's law. Physics calls this the Law of Gravity.

There are other laws we all live by, but most people today are unaware of them. One of the laws is The Law of Cause and Effect. In his book, *The Seven Spiritual Laws of Success*, Deepak Chopra writes, "The Law of Cause and Effect means that every action generates a force of energy that returns to us in like kind… what we sow is what we reap." The Law of Cause and Effect, through our words and actions, has an impact on our experiences and influences the events and outcomes in our life.

So, if we are thinking negative thoughts about how unhappy we are, feeling that we are not good enough, or angry with someone or ourselves, these thoughts and feelings cause actions that eventually bring more feelings of unhappiness, of not being good enough, and more situations that cause us to be angry, upset, or fearful.

Why is it that certain situations in our life work out just fine and other situations do not work out the way we had hoped? How are you feeling about it? Happy, confident, comfortable? Or are you angry, hurt, worried, or fearful? It's all the work of the Law of Cause and Effect. What we sow, we will reap.

According to the Law of Cause and Effect, expressing these feelings through our words or actions is like bursts of energy that go out into our world and eventually return to us. We have an old saying here in the United States, "What goes around, comes around." This is the Law of Cause and Effect in action. By expressing or acting out unfavorable behaviors, we get caught in a cycle of continually experiencing unhappiness and poor results over and over. By expressing positive, uplifting thoughts, feelings, and actions, we can experience the happiness and joy they offer.

The results of our actions don't always happen right away. It can be weeks, months, or maybe even years before we experience a payback or effects. This effect, the experience we have, can be wanted or unwanted, depending on the cause. Divorce or separation from someone can *cause* negative feelings and the *effect* can be stressful experiences. Expressing love for someone can *cause* positive feelings and the *effect* can be uplifting, happy experiences.

What we consume through television, social media, movies and the internet, our family values and religious beliefs, and the people we associate with all have an effect on our thought processes, emotions, belief system, and, ultimately, our behavior. They also have a direct effect on what we experience every day in our life.

If we are angry with someone, we fixate on how angry we are with them. We may talk to someone about the situation and explain why we are angry. This kind of focus makes our anger stronger. Alternately, we hold these feelings inside us, eventually causing disharmony in our body and experiences, which eventually causes us to express this anger through our words, actions, and behavior. It's the same with love. When we are in love with another person, those feelings of love affect our life. Our thoughts, feelings, and behavior grow stronger in positive ways.

What we think, say, and do are a *cause* that produces an *effect* in what happens in our life, the unwanted and wanted. It's the law we live by. That is why we need to live with more awareness of what we are thinking, how we are feeling, and what we are doing. It effects our future.

When we operate at the level of Unaware of What Works, behaving in ways that are not giving us the life we want, the Law of Cause and Effect is NOT working in our favor. We are NOT AWARE that our thoughts and habits from our past conditioning are controlling our lives. However, we can change the course of action by recognizing our behavior, learning how we cause these experiences, and by using the solutions along the path of The Awareness Game.

We are social beings. We want to be involved with others. But when we play out the behaviors shown on the left side of The Chart with others, there is a struggle for control— we play a game of give and take.

In the next section, we will observe how we play out these behaviors and experiences in Conditioned Behavior and see where it leads. Then, we will learn how to use solutions to move out of the games of give and take, and into where we want to be: Playing at What Works.

CONDITIONED BEHAVIOR

The Games of Give and Take

CONDITIONED
BEHAVIOR

Growing up, we were dependent upon the guidance of those who cared for us. Our families, friends, teachers, superiors, and our environment all influenced us every day and every moment. These influences help shape beliefs and behaviors and reinforce certain ideas that have contributed to our learning and personal development so we can live in our environment. But these influences are different for everyone. Therefore, learning and personal development are different for everyone.

We acquire many beliefs during our lifetimes. Beliefs form our opinions and viewpoints, the feelings we have and the conclusions we reach. They help us make decisions about what we want or don't want in our lives. For instance, most of us have a belief that running in front of a moving car is harmful and, therefore, we choose not to do it. Good decision! Or, we could have a belief that eating our favorite ice cream will give us pleasure and, therefore, decide to buy it and eat it. In almost every facet of life, our beliefs influence our behavior and the outcomes.

It all started from the good feelings we got early in life when we were approved of, appreciated, and accepted by others.

Even as a baby, when we got positive attention from our parents, it made us feel good. As we grew up, the way others felt about us had a direct effect on the way we felt about ourselves. When we got attention, we felt loved. *We were accepted.* The more acceptance we got, the better we felt about ourselves, and, pretty soon, we established a belief: "I'm better than others". This belief produced the state from which we operate in our life: doing things to seek more acceptance and feel better about ourselves.

Being accepted—a part of the family and included in the group—has led us to want more of these good feelings. So, we look for ways to be accepted. We behave by excelling at certain things, standing out, taking control of things or people. We expect we will be accepted, approved of, and appreciated for our accomplishments. Seeking acceptance has become an unconscious way of behaving.

The following story will shed light on this type of behavior:

Pete's Story - Once Upon a Time There was a Billionaire

I met him when he was about 39 years old and still working on his first ten million. His greatest asset was that he could see things that other people were not aware of. He could walk rapidly through a factory; go back to the superintendent's office and explain why a certain machine was likely to cause defects in the finished product; spot a sanitation hazard from 200 yards; prove that a certain department was overstaffed by three people.

He could look at the Balance Sheet and Profit and Loss Statement of any company and see ways of dramatically increasing cashflow. In his work with many companies, he could discern which departments were getting the job done, and which departments were more interested in building a hierarchy in a matter of minutes. In a business deal, he could spot opportunities more clearly than his competitor. His joy was beating his business rival. The money was the frosting on the cake.

His real objective was the acceptance he received for a job well done. The way in which he gained this acceptance was through the accumulation of power and control over others.

He could say, "I am successful. I like what I am doing." He knew what he wanted and knew how to get it. He was very creative. He could envision what could be and then make it happen, at least most of the time. He loved what he did. Outsmarting someone always made his day. Of course, he was successful... at least in business.

Could he say, "I have supportive relationships"? In his need to feel superior to those around him, he dominated his associates who feared him; his competitors hated him; his wife ultimately divorced him. He had two sons. One committed suicide and the other moved as far away from his father as possible as soon as he received his trust fund. Did he have supportive relationships with others? It's not likely!

Could he say, "I am satisfied"? He was a driven, short-tempered, stressed, demanding, overbearing man. He shouted and paced anxiously around the floor, chain smoked, and snapped pencils in half. Outside of his business, he had no activities, no hobbies, and no sports interests. Was he filled with a sense of satisfaction, happiness, contentment, and wellbeing? I hardly think so!

Could he say, "I am secure"? Power, authority, controlling others, and being better than others was the source of his security, but the fear of losing his power was ever present. He ran for a high public office position. He spent millions more than his opponents. He was sure he would win. He was defeated in the party primaries. He found out that he was not as powerful as he'd thought. He did not get the recognition he was sure he deserved. Could power have slipped away from him? Was he free from uncertainty or free from fear of the future? Was he really secure? It's doubtful!

The billionaire managed to acquire success in business because he knew how to stay focused on the results he wanted. Support from others was difficult because he controlled people and the outcomes. Satisfaction was not a motivation to him. Achieving a result and being recognized for it was more important. Financial security wasn't important because he knew how to make money. His security came from the recognition and acceptance he received because of his business successes and accomplishments. Did he have a balanced life? Not likely!

The billionaire began his journey by believing he was better than others. This caused him to behave in certain ways: taking charge, and dominating and controlling others, the situation, or the outcome. This was all for the pleasurable experience of being recognized, approved of, or accepted for his successes.

It doesn't have to be this way. You don't have to give up caring about people, your health, or your security to be successful. You can learn how to make a life that will give you balance and happiness as well as success just by using the principles of *The Awareness Game*.

> **Another way our beliefs influence our behavior is when we do something or agree to something we don't want to avoid stressful feelings or rejection.**

It started at a time when we did something we shouldn't have done. Perhaps when we were very young, we were punished or had feelings of hurt or guilt. When we did something wrong, we felt rejected, put down, left out, or unloved. We felt that we were not good enough. We felt we had failed because our behavior was not acceptable. So, we established the belief: "I'm not good enough." This belief has become an unconscious state in which we operate in our lives. We avoid disappointment, resistance, resentment, or rejection from others at all cost.

Those who worked for the billionaire... how do you think they felt giving into his demands or abuse? They might have been demoted or lost their jobs if they hadn't given in. Now ask yourself: how many times in your life have you compromised your values for a promise of something or to avoid feeling as though you're not good enough?

We have all done it.

When walking the path of Conditioned Behavior, we express both behaviors that have become unconscious motives—silent motivating forces—that control our lives. Sometimes we feel that we're better than others, and we search for the attention and acceptance which that brings. Other times, when we are not feeling good enough, we make decisions or do things to avoid the disappointment we think might follow.

However, when we seek acceptance or avoid rejection, these motives and the behaviors caused by them produce unwanted outcomes at the expense of self-esteem, satisfaction, and personal freedom. These motives become our driving force instead of the desired outcome. Constantly seeking acceptance or avoiding rejection causes behaviors that are hidden to us—unconscious behavior. In the end, these motives will result in the cycle of Conditioned Behavior where unwanted experiences occur over and over. They will not promote success, support, satisfaction, or the security you want.

Pete and I lived through all the behaviors shown on the path of Conditioned Behavior. Our relationship was volatile for the first few years of our marriage. We were playing the game of give and take. We were living out Conditioned Behaviors acquired from our past relationships and in other parts of our life. But the Awareness Game Chart was always present, showing us what we were doing.

It was uncomfortable. I was scared. I didn't know what I wanted at the time. I ran away. Pete and I divorced. Was this another failure? Read on.

Why did I put up with situations in my life that were less than satisfactory? Why did I need to control everything and everyone in my life? Why did I allow myself to be emotionally damaged by others? Why did I allow myself to be a victim of stress? Fear? Anger? Guilt? Conditioned Behavior was running my life. I was unaware of how I caused the resulting consequences.

I needed to make some major changes to my thought processes and my feelings of anger over my struggle to work and raise my children on my own. I needed to pay attention to my behavior and stop making decisions and agreeing with others just so I could gain or avoid something. I had to discover what I wanted from my life. I went to work on myself.

I used the solutions and principles of The Awareness Game to gain clarity about where I wanted to be and the direction of my life. In doing so, my outcomes started changing.

The time had come to take responsibility for my life, and six months later Pete and I remarried. We walked over the Bridge of Courage, shown on The Chart, started Playing At What Works, and cleared up the past. I will explain how we did this.

Remember the Law of Cause and Effect? "What we sow is what we reap." It's always operating in our lives. Seeking acceptance and avoiding rejection causes habits of behavior that put into motion the cycle of Conditioned Behavior, a cycle in which we keep experiencing unsatisfactory outcomes. What we cause comes back to us in the experiences we have.

When you are experiencing the discomfort of Conditioned Behavior—feeling like your life is stuck and experiencing the same poor results over and over—it's time to wake up to a new reality. Look at what you are doing and ask yourself why you are doing it. Are your results what you want? Is there an unconscious belief or motive hiding in your mind and standing in your way? Learn how you are influencing the outcomes and make changes before your life gets out of control which will lead to disharmony and unsatisfactory results, if it hasn't already.

Having control over your life is what you are aiming for. *Taking control* over someone else's life, their behaviors, and decisions, can't and won't work. You can't change other people, no matter how hard you try. You can only change yourself.

Similarly, you can't *give up control* to others, either. Why not? Because you will lose your freedom of choice, which eventually leads to other behaviors on the path of Conditioned Behavior: compromising your values, justifying your position when things aren't working out, and not taking responsibility for what happens to you.

It's important to note that walking the path of Conditioned Behavior is a struggle. It's a barrier to the fulfillment of your purpose and to where you want to be in your life.

The next part of Conditioned Behavior, the game of give and take with others, will help you recognize when you are expressing unconscious behaviors that are standing in the way of achieving more successful outcomes. There is a path from False Agreement to The Pits when operating at Conditioned Behavior. The path can be quick or can take years to develop through the games of give and take. It depends on the situation and the people involved. However, when you find yourself acting out any of the behaviors in Unaware of What Works or Discovering What Works, you can quickly get out by using the appropriate solutions along the path. There is more to come on this.

The Chart shows four types of games played in Conditioned Behavior. Each game has two players. The players on The Chart are non-gendered personalities or characters expressing behaviors that you will recognize when you see them.

The motive for the player in the *red toga* is to seek acceptance, approval, recognition, or importance. Their behavior is to *take control of others, a situation or outcome, usually at the expense of others.*

The motive for the player in the *orange toga* is to avoid being rejected or feeling unworthy or not smart enough. The behavior is to *give in or give up control to others, a situation, or outcome, usually at the expense of yourself.*

We can play either role with different people or in different situations. It depends on our past conditioning and interests, and our self-confidence and motivation, or lack thereof in each situation. For instance, you can express Red's behavior with your family and Orange's behavior at work. But, in the long run, these unconscious behaviors can ruin your life, and will produce unsatisfactory results whether you are taking control or giving up control to others, situations, or outcomes.

In the beginning of my relationship with Pete, I mostly acted out the unconscious behaviors of the Red Toga. After all, for years I had to make decisions for myself, my family, and work. I knew what was best, or so I thought.

Pete played the Orange Toga most of the time. He believed his family loved his brother best and felt he was not good enough. We were a good match for playing the games of give and take, at least for a while. Unaware of What Works developed out of experiencing our relationship together and observing our results, as well as observing the behaviors and results of others. Through this awareness, our life together got better.

When you look at The Chart, you see each game of give and take is part of a drama that begins with making a False Agreement—an agreement based on a result or outcome that has the goal of seeking acceptance or avoiding rejection instead of accomplishing an agreeable outcome in which all will benefit. When results are not being achieved as expected, the path ahead escalates and becomes more uncomfortable. It can end in the tragedy of The Pits. We then go back to the cycle of Conditioned Behavior and begin or continue the games of give and take with other people. Alternately, The Pits can be the motivator to trigger us to look at the results we are getting and the beliefs and motives that cause our behavior, so we can change what isn't working.

Awareness of our beliefs and motives is the way out of Conditioned Behavior. Reflect on what is driving you to do the things which result in disharmony and discomfort. When you recognize your motives and change your beliefs, your behavior changes as well do your outcomes. This is a process that moves you out of the past and brings you into the present where you have an opportunity to live your life with more conscious control and awareness.

I feel I know so much more now than when I married Pete in 1981. I had to use The Awareness Game Chart to look at the beliefs and motives that were driving me and recognize how I was causing my own experiences. I was living my life in Conditioned Behavior. I used the solutions and The Game Plan, which you'll learn about soon, to make changes in my life. Now I see it was worth it. I feel so much better about myself and more in charge of my life. If I can do it, you can do it too.

Let's take a look at The Chart and see how your beliefs and underlying motives play out in real life so you can recognize these behaviors when they happen. Only then will you learn how to use the solutions to move out of the cycle of Conditioned Behavior and towards Playing At What Works. We will start at False Agreement.

FALSE AGREEMENT
Seeking Acceptance or Avoiding Rejection

TAKING CONTROL
TO BE ACCEPTED

GIVING IN TO
AVOID REJECTION

FALSE AGREEMENT

FALSE AGREEMENT

False Agreement is the beginning of Conditioned Behavior. As we explored in the previous section, when agreeing on an outcome with others the motive is to either seek acceptance or to avoid rejection by doing what others want you to do. Either behavior is usually at the expense of yourself or others.

The billionaire wanted control of everything he was involved in because he believed if others did it his way the job would get done "right", and he would be accepted and recognized for the successes he sought. The people who worked for the billionaire gave into his demands because if they did what he wanted they would get paid and would also avoid any possible rejection or failure if things went "wrong".

We see this behavior in many relationships, too. Sometimes, we make friends with certain people to be part of a group and be involved, included, and accepted. Some people get married for security instead of love. Perhaps they have good intentions when they marry, but after a while there's conflict. This often ends with a desire that was not fulfilled. They wanted to gain something or avoid something that was not known or agreed upon when the relationship began. This is False Agreement.

How do you know when you are making a False Agreement? It's very subtle. However, you can usually identify a False Agreement when your results are not turning out as you think they should.

False Agreements can be written or made through verbal consent. They can also be non-verbal—a handshake—or assumed. For instance, you may have a discussion with someone and assume they are willing to participate, but this assumption can set up an unsatisfactory outcome. When this happens ask yourself, "Did I agree to be involved with someone under the assumption I would gain something in return? Or was I avoiding something that was, or could be, uncomfortable?" These motives will never produce the results you want without friction.

If the results are not what you wanted or expected, this is a sign. When you are involved with others, be aware of whether your motives and behaviors are benefiting you and others. What role are you playing: the red toga or the orange toga? By recognizing your role, you will be relieved from the discomfort that is waiting for you further along the path of Conditioned Behavior.

Let's look at the left side of The Chart—False Agreement:

The Red Toga - *Taking control of others, a situation or outcome.*

While our results may be desirable ones, they are not as important as the recognition, appreciation, respect, approval, and other good feelings we will receive for doing something and succeeding at it. In the past, we have done many things for acceptance, and the reward of having others see us as a good and successful person made us feel good. We've learned that **taking control** of an outcome, a situation, or others is worthwhile.

The Orange Toga - *Giving in to others, a situation or outcome.*

Early in life we found that when we did what others wanted us to do, we belonged, we were included, and we were part of a group. On the other hand, we learned that if we resisted doing what others wanted us to do, we could be punished, criticized, disapproved of or rejected. So, we **gave in** to others. We did it their way and seemingly avoided rejection and the uncomfortable feelings that would have come from it.

Both Players have this in common: they believe they'll get what they want and think the result will make them feel good or better about themselves. "If I **take control** of the situation and get the job done, I will gain the acceptance I deserve." The other player believes, "If I **give in** and do what is expected of me, I will look good and avoid rejection or any hurtful feelings caused by others." Both believe they are in a winning situation. That is until the results are not as they planned.

Look at the billionaire who was surrounded all his life by people who did things his way in the hopes of avoiding his rejection and maintaining their employment. The billionaire was powerful. He promised great benefits if you were associated with him. As long as you did things his way, you were accepted. But if you did things any other way, you were immediately rejected.

There is nothing wrong with wanting to gain something as long as it is not harming or taking something away from yourself or others. Growing and becoming a more aware person, being a better person, and treating others as you want to be treated, with respect and understanding, is what you need to do. We are all in this life together. Becoming a better person is a lifelong journey. Our personal development, growth, and awareness benefits others through our knowledge and example. When we are more aware and caring, others follow our example. It's the law.

The Game of False Agreement creates unsatisfactory experiences because each person involved has an ulterior motive or unspoken desire, either to gain something (usually at someone else's expense) or avoid something (usually at their expense). You are not being clear or focused in the agreement you made, whether verbal or assumed. Your motive of seeking acceptance or avoiding rejection is getting in the way of the outcome you both agreed upon.

This game can go on as long as both players choose to put up with it, but sooner or later attitudes change. Both players assumed or planned on something happening, but that "something" fails to materialize. This creates a problem and begins to strain relationships. So, the drama intensifies. It's a crisis in the making.

Unless you recognize the behavior early on, sometime in the future you will move to the Game of Forced Agreement. This is the next spot on the path of Conditioned Behavior that we cover in the next chapter.

When you recognize this behavior early, you can move directly to The Game Plan and use the first principle: Be Clear. Focus on desirable results that benefit all involved. You will learn about this principle when we discuss What Works.

FORCED AGREEMENT

Manipulating and Compromising

COMPROMISING
TO AVOID
REJECTION

MANIPULATING
TO STAY IN
CONTROL

FORCED
AGREEMENT

FORCED AGREEMENT

The Game of Forced Agreement begins when agreements are not happening as planned. Forced Agreement is a power struggle for control, a win-lose situation between the Red and Orange togas.

Forced Agreement is easier to recognize. You can hear the words or feel the implication: "If you do something, you'll get something."

Red Toga - *Taking Control of others, a situation or outcome*

You want to get back in control of a situation that is not working out as you'd planned. Your method for gaining control is manipulation. You appeal to the possible fear others have of failure, rejection, pain, or survival. You promise success or threaten with failure. You promise support or threaten with rejection. You promise pleasure or threaten with pain. You promise money or threaten to take it away. In short, you do whatever works to get back in control.

What you don't realize is that each time you "win" the game of Forced Agreement, you learn that you cannot trust people. Their behavior or work must be scrutinized. Each time you take on the responsibility of controlling people, you put yourself at the mercy of others rather than being free to enjoy the things you want to be doing.

But you think it's worth it. Each time you are successful, the basis of your power becomes more secure, you become more confident, and you gain more acceptance, approval, and recognition. Or so you think!

Orange Toga - *Giving In to others, a situation or outcome*

You are unable or unwilling to continue to do what you are doing or to complete the agreements you may have made. You probably didn't want to do it in the first place, but the thought of being involved and the successful outcome appealed to you.

However, because you are not as powerful, in the face of promises and threats you find yourself at the mercy of what could happen if you refused. Through this, you compromise your values. You give in to the manipulation of others.

But you think it's worth it. If you succeed by doing it someone else's way people will see you as a good person and you will avoid disapproval or rejection. You resist the manipulation but eventually compromise against your wishes.

Look at the billionaire constantly having to control those around him. He thought he was surrounded by managers and employees far less competent than him but, in reality, his gains were a hostile marriage, resentful children, and a 16-hour-day workload. He definitely took control. He knew what was best for everyone even though he was unaware it was at the expense of his stress levels, health, and supportive relationships.

And what about those who gave in to the billionaire? They allowed themselves to be used or taken advantage of because they would get something in return that would make them feel good about themselves.

The Game of Forced Agreement can be played many times in different situations and with many people involved at the same time. It is an unconscious habit of behavior. You do not see yourself behaving this way, unless you pay attention.

When you do recognize your behavior during this time, you can easily move out of the situation by using the second principle of The Game Plan—Be Fair. You will learn about that soon. Obtain support by satisfying the concerns of all involved. This allows everyone to gain a clear understanding of what's involved so you can make informed decisions that support the interests and desires of everyone.

Without paying attention to your behavior, this kind of game gets the best of both the Red and Orange players. At the end of this round, there is going to be a power struggle; a struggle for control. The drama intensifies and tempers flare as you move up the path to Disagreement.

DISAGREEMENT
Blaming and Justifying

DISAGREEMENT

The Game of Disagreement begins when your expectations or results are once again not being met. Disagreement is a power struggle that has gone out of control, a lose-lose situation between Red and Orange toga. Disagreement starts out like Forced Agreement, but this time you both think you are right but no one gets what they want.

Red Toga - *Taking control of others, a situation or outcome*

Once again you are getting results that are not as you expected. Agreements you thought you had with people are not being fulfilled to your liking. You are angry and you are not going to tolerate the situation any longer.

Your method to maintain control is to make others wrong, to blame them for things not working out as you planned. Confrontation is coming. You deliver the list of offenses that have been committed and blame the failure on others. But, since you don't want to admit defeat and still want to win, you are willing to continue with your plan and want others to change their ways and do it your way. You think about the acceptance you will get for this kind of perseverance.

The hidden problem here is that you believe you are just trying to work things out, but the real objective is to avoid taking responsibility for what isn't working: your behavior and your actions. You blame others because you believe you are right.

Orange Toga - *Giving In to others, a situation or outcome*

You were manipulated into making an agreement you were unwilling or unable to keep. Now, you are being blamed for what isn't working. You are angry and are not going to take it any longer. You are tired of being bullied. Even though you want to avoid confrontation, you justify your actions with why things didn't work out. You come up with a whole list of reasons why it was okay for you to do what you did or didn't do.

You believe that you are just trying to explain your actions but your objective, in this situation, is to avoid taking any responsibility for what isn't working—your behavior and actions. You want to avoid being rejected, feeling like a bad person or being wrong. But this avoidance means you have once again focused on the unwanted result rather than your agreements and contributing to the outcome. You were not being truthful to yourself or others about what you could or would do.

You might feel guilty for selling out, but your yearning for happiness is now stronger than your need to avoid rejection and other uncomfortable feelings. You no longer want to be involved or controlled by others.

In this game, communication has broken down. Neither player is getting the result that was originally wanted. The desire to seek acceptance, power, recognition, or approval has been replaced with the need to get rid of the burden created by others. The desire to avoid rejection has been replaced with resentment and a desire to get even for being manipulated or used in the first place. You both believe you are right, but neither of you get what you want.

Look at the stress in the billionaire's life. A son's suicide. A divorce from his wife. Political defeat. But did he blame himself? Could he be wrong? Of course not. He blamed others. And those who couldn't take his abuse any longer, were they wrong? Neither the Red Toga nor Orange Toga are getting the results they hoped for.

The struggle for control has now reached an impasse. Both sides are in a defensive position, which is completely justified in their minds. If you recognize this behavior now, you can change the outcome by using the third principle of The Game Plan—Be Truthful. Make agreements you can and will keep. Then, everyone can build trust in each other and allow positive results to happen. You will learn about this soon.

Or this game is almost over and the players will eventually move to the next step: the drama of the Game of Separation.

SEPARATION

It's Your Fault. It's Not My Fault.

SEPARATION

The Game of Separation is a game of failure. In this game both players get the same outcome. No one has achieved the results, appreciation, understanding, or benefits they'd sought. No one is taking responsibility for what happened because they feel they were right, or that they were wronged. They believe it was not their fault. Both players have given up. Relationships have suffered. Confidence has been damaged. Creativity has been stifled. Most of all, no one has found a solution to the problem or achieved the original outcome they'd wanted.

Red Toga - *Taking control of others, a situation or outcome*

You have separated from the other and are no longer involved in the situation. You believe the failure to achieve the outcome you wanted is someone else's fault. So, you get to be right, but you also fail to get what you wanted.

Orange Toga - *Giving in to others, a situation or outcome*

You have been wronged. You have been accused or rejected because of something that wasn't your fault. You can hold onto this position but you didn't get what you wanted, either.

As long as both players can convince themselves that what happened was not their fault, they will move onto the next phase of Conditioned Behavior: The Pits.

But, again, you have the choice to make a change right now. You can use the fourth principle of The Game Plan – Be Responsible - which you will learn about later. Complete your agreements and evaluate the results along the way. Make appropriate changes that support the desired outcome as well as the people involved. This way, everyone is working towards the same objective, and everyone wins.

Separation happens all the time. Someone gets divorced or fired from their job. People leave friendships due to arguments. However, holding onto the position that you were right or that you were wronged is not how to get what you want.

Look at the billionaire. Lonely, reflecting on a life full of family and people who have let him down and haven't lived up to his expectations. But was it his fault? Or was it the fault of all those people who didn't do their part and were trying to take advantage of him? What do you think?

Now, let's take a look at the inevitable conclusion of playing the games of give and take: the drama of The Pits.

THE PITS
Despair

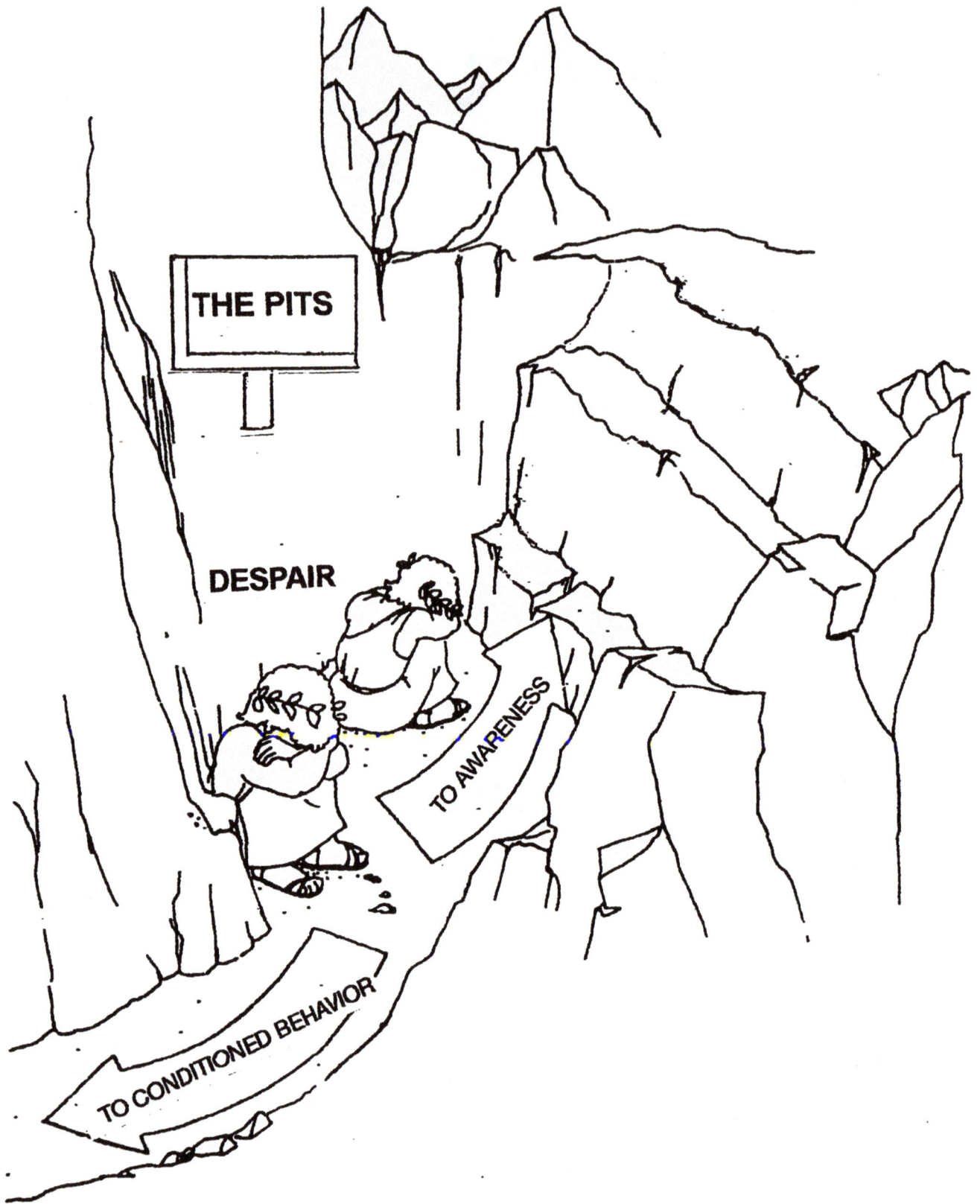

THE PITS

So how did we get here? Conditioned Behavior starts with False Agreement. This is when you agree to something for acceptance or to avoid rejection. When things aren't working out according to your plans, the path ahead is Forced Agreement. This is where you either control others, the situation or the outcome through manipulation, or you make concessions by compromising your values and wants. Then, when the poor results continue, Disagreement begins. You blame others to justify things that aren't working out, which inevitably results in Separation because you believe that what happened was not your fault.

All of this culminates in the inevitable drama of The Pits.

Here's an example of how you got there. The solution is coming.

Red and Orange start a business together. They agree on an outcome. Red will manage the business and Orange will manage sales and marketing. They will split the profits.

Is there False Agreement at this time? It is hard to say at this point. A False Agreement is mostly an unconscious habit that drives people from the inside rather than something overtly shown on the outside as a behavior. The deep inner motive may not be known to either Orange or Red. Alternatively, it might only be known to one of them but not expressed at this time.

Everything goes well for a while. Then, Red thinks the results are not happening the way they should and wants more from Orange. Red starts wanting Orange to change a behavior or do something differently to improve profits. Orange wants to avoid any confrontation and discomfort, so he gives into Red's request to change what he is doing. The agreement is in place, or at least Red thinks so, but manipulating and compromising behavior has just occurred. Forced Agreement is in play. Red starts taking charge and watches over Orange's work and behavior with a critical eye. This behavior can go on for months or years.

Orange is doing his best, or so Orange thinks. Red expects more. Requests have now turned into demands. When Orange doesn't meet the demands, Red starts blaming Orange for not doing what he expected him to do. Sales are falling and marketing strategies don't seem to be working. Orange justifies a position to avoid being wrong. This argument strains the relationship but business must go on. This is Disagreement.

Things are still not working out according to Red's plans. Red is tired of Orange not doing the job as expected: not changing and not doing what's best for the company in order to make the profit Red expects. Red wants out of the relationship. Orange is tired of being bullied and also wants out. Red tells Orange, "It's your fault for things not working out. You didn't do your part or what you agreed to do." Orange tells Red, "It's not my fault" and offers one excuse after another. Red and Orange part ways. This is Separation and a failure for both.

The Pits is the final destination for Red and Orange. Each has had their own emotionally painful experience and now they each have a choice to make. They could ignore the negative feelings found in The Pits and go on their way to the next experience, continuing their Unconscious Behavior and playing the games of give and take with others. Alternatively, each of them could choose to become aware of how their motives and behavior has caused the failed experience they have had.

The Pits can be the most important experience you have. It can also be emotionally painful. When you fall into The Pits, there can be feelings of despair, sadness, sorrow, hopelessness, helplessness, grief, guilt, depression and even a desire to get even.

But you don't want to remain in The Pits because hanging onto those emotions will keep you trapped there. Luckily, there are two ways out: Back to Conditioned Behavior or Climbing Out of The Pits.

The Path Back to Conditioned Behavior

Both Red and Orange believe they are "right". If you get acknowledgment from others that what you have done in this situation was right, eventually that confirmation will land you back in Conditioned Behavior where you will begin the cycle of give and take all over again in another situation with someone else.

You get to hold onto your position, beliefs, and motives. You get to be right, but you don't get what you want. You will go back to playing the game of give and take and experiencing unsatisfactory situations repeatedly. This is the cycle of Conditioned Behavior. This will continue until you learn how you are responsible for the outcomes in your life.

We see this behavior all the time—in our movies and TV series, on the news, in our failed relationships and even in the history of wars and battles between states and countries. There is a power struggle to maintain the position of "I am right" or "we are right" that adds more destruction and failure to our lives.

But it's time to change this behavior and be kind to one another instead of criticizing or proving others "wrong", which is essentially forcing them to be a certain way or do something our way.

Here is a saying about stopping to think before you speak. It's called The Three Gates. There is much speculation on the internet regarding who shared this wisdom. Regardless, when we stop and answer these questions before we speak they can open our hearts and uplift our outcomes. Practicing this simple technique can help us to speak and act in a way that includes others and brings about harmony.

The Three Gates
Ask yourself first before you speak:
Is it true?
Is it necessary?
Is it kind?

You can stay in The Pits for a long time. The games of give and take can last weeks, months, or years before making you weary of the unsatisfactory experiences you are having. The Pits naturally holds negative feelings. These feelings can continue to build because you have a position to maintain. *You were right* or *you were wronged.* This leads you back to Conditioned Behavior. Going back to Conditioned Behavior won't provide more comfort because The Law of Cause and Effect is not working in your favor. What you put out in words and actions will come back to you at some time, in some way. This behavior is what led you to The Pits.

Conditioned Behavior started with an ulterior motive—making a False Agreement. Were you seeking to gain something (power, approval, recognition, acceptance)? Were you feeling better than others? Or were you avoiding rejection or the negative feeling of not being good enough? Cause and Effect is always working and when you operate from Conditioned Behavior you will not produce the desired outcomes. What you are causing comes back to you in form of future experiences.

Listen to the words you use and the emotions you are feeling and expressing. Pay attention to your behavior and the actions you are taking. They will eventually come back to you from other people or other situations.

Pete and I played the games of give and take for a while. It wasn't easy to look at my behavior and realize I wasn't being clear about what I wanted, not only in my own life but in my life with Pete. Pete and I repeatedly fell into Conditioned Behavior and often occupied The Pits. That's why Conditioned Behavior has been presented to you on The Chart as a visual path. We know where it will eventually lead. We have experienced it and, I'm guessing, so have you.

Life does not have to be a game of give and take. There is no need to control other people or everything around you. There is no need to give up control of your life to other people, either. When both players are clear about what they want, fair with each other, truthful about what they can and will do, and responsible for the outcome, it can be a game of **Offer and Accept** where agreements and results are mutually satisfactory. That's what The Game Plan is all about: playing a Game of Offer and Accept.

You have a choice right now. You can continue to play the games of give and take and return to unsatisfactory experiences and struggle over and over or you can use the solution for Climbing Out of The Pits and take the path toward greater happiness.

Now, let's move on to Part II: Discovering What Works - Climbing Out of The Pits.

Part II

DISCOVERING WHAT WORKS
Learning Experiences

DISCOVERING WHAT WORKS

Discovering What Works offers the solutions for Climbing Out of The Pits and for Moving Through Pit Stop #2.

Nature has a wonderful way of helping us see what isn't working. It gives us a learning experience; an opportunity to know how we cause our experiences. When we learned to walk, we took it a few steps at a time and may have fallen several times before we got the hang of it. This was not failure but a learning experience. We learned what worked and what didn't work.

When we were children and young adults, we went to school to learn the basics to get along in the world. We learned to read and comprehend words and symbols, calculate numbers and equations, the history of our environment and the cosmos, and how to use language to express ourselves. These are learning experiences that continue to help us grow into better beings but learning from our past misunderstandings or failures does this as well.

Look at past outcomes and evaluate what has worked and what hasn't worked. This will prevent future mistakes and stressful experiences. Learning means growing, becoming better at what you do and better at how you communicate.

Below is a marvelous Sufi story about a wise old farmer who had learned to look at misfortunes as learning experiences that were really helping him.

The Farmer and The Neighbor

One day, while the farmer was plowing his field, his horse broke loose from the plow and ran away. That night, the neighbor came over to commiserate with the farmer over his loss. Over and over, the neighbor told the farmer how sorry he was that the farmer was doomed for the rest of his days to take the place of the horse and pull the plow. How sorry he was that without the horse, they would not have enough food. How sorry he was for the pain and agony the farmer would have to endure. He went on and on and on. The farmer replied, "Who knows what is good or bad?"

The next day, to everyone's surprise, the horse returned leading a band of 20 wild horses. That night, the neighbor came over to congratulate the farmer on his good fortune. How wonderful that this should happen to a man who had such a good friend as himself, the neighbor. How wonderful that it should happen to a man who was known for his generosity and his desire to share his wealth with those less fortunate, and on and on and on. The farmer replied, "Who knows what is good or bad?"

The next day, the farmer's son broke his leg while trying to ride one of the wild horses. That night, the neighbor came over to express his sorrow. The broken leg might not heal. There was the risk of gangrene. The farmer might lose his son and not have an heir to inherit the family name, and on and on and on. To which, the farmer replied, "Who knows what is good or bad?"

And sure enough, the next day, the Emperor's soldiers came to conscript men for the army as they did about every ten years but because the farmer's son had a broken leg, they did not take him. They took the neighbor instead.

When you see your misfortunes as failures, you become uncertain and fearful of the future. You will be prone to playing the games of give and take—seeking acceptance or avoiding rejection, manipulating others or compromising your values, blaming others or justifying your actions and, eventually, criticizing others and separating from them. However, when you see your misfortunes as learning experiences which help to promote success for all involved, you are seeing things clearly. You are Playing at What Works.

Many people don't want to question their motives or look at their beliefs or behavior. Either they feel they are right in what they've done or are doing or they want to avoid any bad feelings that might arise from admitting they are responsible for causing their experience. But when you observe your past behavior and recognize your reasons for it, you can release the burden and stress it causes in your life. You are free to move on and become better at changing, improving, and creating rewarding outcomes.

There is no shame or guilt involved in admitting you were wrong, made a mistake, or were involved in an unsatisfactory experience. We have all played the game of give and take and fallen into The Pits. Humans are not perfect. We have all had to pay the price in some way and have experienced the hard knocks and emotional dramas which come with Conditioned Behavior. This is part of our past. Let it go. It's time to experience a different now.

By recognizing your involvement you will begin to change your beliefs, your motives, and your behavior; this will lead to better outcomes along your way in life. Understand what is causing unsatisfactory experiences. Learn from it. Move on to a productive and happier life. Having a learning experience is an opportunity to get out of the emotional cycle of Conditioned Behavior and move away from unpleasant experiences.

There are two ways out of The Pits. You can go back to Conditioned Behavior and continue the cycle all over again with someone else and in another situation. Alternatively, you can understand your beliefs and past motives, recognize the behaviors caused by them, learn how you were involved, and then move on to desirable outcomes.

When you recognize your deep inner motive and the behavior caused by it, you will understand how you were involved in *causing* the experience that produced the *effect* you had. With this understanding, you can be on the lookout for thoughts, feelings, beliefs and behaviors that are not supporting a desirable outcome.

When you are Discovering What Works, you are at a much higher level of awareness because you are willing to learn and understand how you contribute to your experiences. This knowledge can help with future decisions and actions, and lead to much better outcomes.

CLIMBING OUT OF THE PITS

An Aha Moment

MOTIVES AND BEHAVIOR
ARE THE CAUSE

TO AWARENESS

USE THE KEYS

CLIMBING OUT OF THE PITS

Failure is an opportunity to get out of the cycle of Conditioned Behavior and move out of an emotionally unpleasant experience. It's uncomfortable in The Pits. Is that what you want?

Let's learn what led you to The Pits, and how you can climb out.

Use The Keys to Awareness below to Climb Out of The Pits and feel the relief and freedom it gives your thoughts, emotions, and overall wellbeing. As an added bonus, the more you learn about yourself, the more understanding and compassion you will feel for others going through the same struggle as you.

Since we can play both roles in Conditioned Behavior—seeking acceptance and avoiding rejection— in different situations and with different people, picking your motive depends on which Toga you were wearing. Were you wearing the Red Toga, feeling like you were better than others and wanting to control the situation? Or were you wearing the Orange Toga, feeling as though you were not good enough and giving up control in some way?

Let's explore the path to see where we end up. We will go backwards from Separation to False Agreement in order to understand how your motives and behavior led you to The Pits.

The Keys to Awareness

The Problem:

• **What was the experience or outcome that caused my unfortunate fall into The Pits?**

_____

_____

_____

• **What role did I play in this situation?**

_____**Red Toga - Taking Control**

If you are trying to take control over others, a situation or the outcome, it is likely your motivation to seek acceptance is overriding the desired results.

Separation - I believed the unsatisfactory outcome was someone else's fault.

Disagreement - I blamed others for things not working the way I thought it should.

Forced Agreement - I promised something or threatened to take it away.

False Agreement - I wanted something more for myself than the desired outcome (importance, approval, recognition, acceptance from others).

_____**Orange Toga - Giving In or Giving Up Control**

If you are giving in to others, it is likely your motivation to avoid rejection is overriding the desired result.

Separation - I believed the unsatisfactory outcome was not my fault.

Disagreement - I justified my position when things weren't working out.

Forced Agreement - I compromised my wants or needs in order to avoid being wrong.

False Agreement - I avoided something by giving in to others at the expense of myself (rejection, feeling not good or smart enough).

- **What was my motive for being involved in the first place? Was I looking for acceptance from others by taking control of the situation or was I avoiding rejection by giving in to this situation?** You only have to admit it to yourself before your motivation and behaviors start to change and strengthen your character. It all started with a False Agreement.

_____

_____

_____

When you are feeling discomfort or as if things did not work out as planned: STOP. BREATHE. ASK.

What was the unfortunate outcome? What was my behavior? Why did I behave that way? Was I feeling better than others or not good enough? This recognition will provide the understanding necessary to change or improve what isn't working. Be aware of the choices, decisions and agreements you make with yourself and others. This awareness will bring more insight when you behave in this way in the future. When this insight happens, it's a benefit to you. You are becoming more aware, more conscious, more present. Soon, Conditioned Behavior will decrease and eventually stop running your life.

Think about what the future will bring you. You're learning from each of your experiences along the way, improving respect and compassion for yourself and others, and leading the life you want with more and more successes. You're growing, becoming a better person, and including other people with a clearer understanding of their life journey.

We need to interact with others to learn more about ourselves. That's how we develop our character and grow as individuals. So, why not take the opportunity to make this the best life ever?

After you recognize your motive and how Conditioned Behavior was involved in causing your experiences, you can walk through the light-filled arch on The Chart and go directly to The Bridge of Courage.

MOVING THROUGH PIT STOP #2

Another Aha Moment

PIT STOP #2

What's different about being in The Pits or Pit Stop #2? The emotions and behavior expressed are different. In The Pits, feelings and behaviors were expressed outwardly towards other people. The Pits was caused by a deep inner motive that caused stressful behaviors along the path of Conditioned Behavior.

Pit Stop #2 is the result of something not working out after you've applied The Game Plan principles to something you'd wanted to achieve. The emotions felt in Pit Stop #2 are not expressed outwardly towards others. Instead, there's an inward experience of hurt, disappointment, or confusion. You thought you were doing all the right things by following The Game Plan, but what you'd expected to happen didn't. Something is not working. Welcome to Pit Stop #2.

Moving through Pit Stop #2

Pit Stop #2 is a higher level of awareness, and it is temporary. You understand that life is a series of learning experiences leading to more successful outcomes but, right now, things aren't working out as you'd expected. You are not getting the support or satisfaction you had thought you would.

At its core, this is an opportunity to learn how expectations can cause hurt feelings and unsatisfactory outcomes that can stand in your way.

Red Toga - You are not getting the support from others that you had expected. You know you've been doing the very best you can. You used the principles of The Game Plan. You thought you were clear about the outcome and your motive was to participate and succeed but, right now, it doesn't seem to be worth the effort. Your results are not what you were expecting them to be. You are not getting support from others. You are feeling hurt and disappointed.

Orange Toga - Again, things are not working. You know you cause your experiences but, this time, you can't see what you are doing wrong. You used the principles of The Game Plan. You thought you were clear about the outcome and your motive had been to participate and succeed. But your results are not what you'd expected. You are not feeling supported. You are upset and confused.

This experience is happening so you can learn something you need to know about yourself. Just like learning anything new, it takes practice to develop your new skill. With practice, you will become better at using The Game Plan. The more you use it, the more you learn about how to be clear about the result, fair with those involved, truthful about what's to be done and responsible for the outcome. Over time, The Game Plan will contribute to better and more successes.

It's time to discover what led you to Pit Stop #2. Use The Formula below to move out of Pit Stop #2 and learn how your expectations caused an unwanted experience.

The Formula

Evaluate the situation:

• **What did I expect would happen?**

_____

_____

_____

• **How did others contribute to the problem?**

_____

_____

_____

• **How did I contribute to the problem?**

_____

_____

_____

_____Was I unclear about the outcome?

_____Was I unfair with those involved?

_____Was I untruthful about what I could and would do?

_____Was I irresponsible about my part in the result?

_____Did I evaluate the results along the way?

_____Did I make new agreements when necessary?

- **How was I responsible for the unwanted outcome?**

_____

_____

_____

Keep asking these questions until the answers become clear to you. Having unfulfilled expectations just means you are learning a new skill. Once you understand how your contribution, or lack of contribution, caused the unwanted experience in Pit Stop #2, go directly to the Bridge of Courage.

Part III

PLAYING AT WHAT WORKS
Experiencing More Successful Outcomes

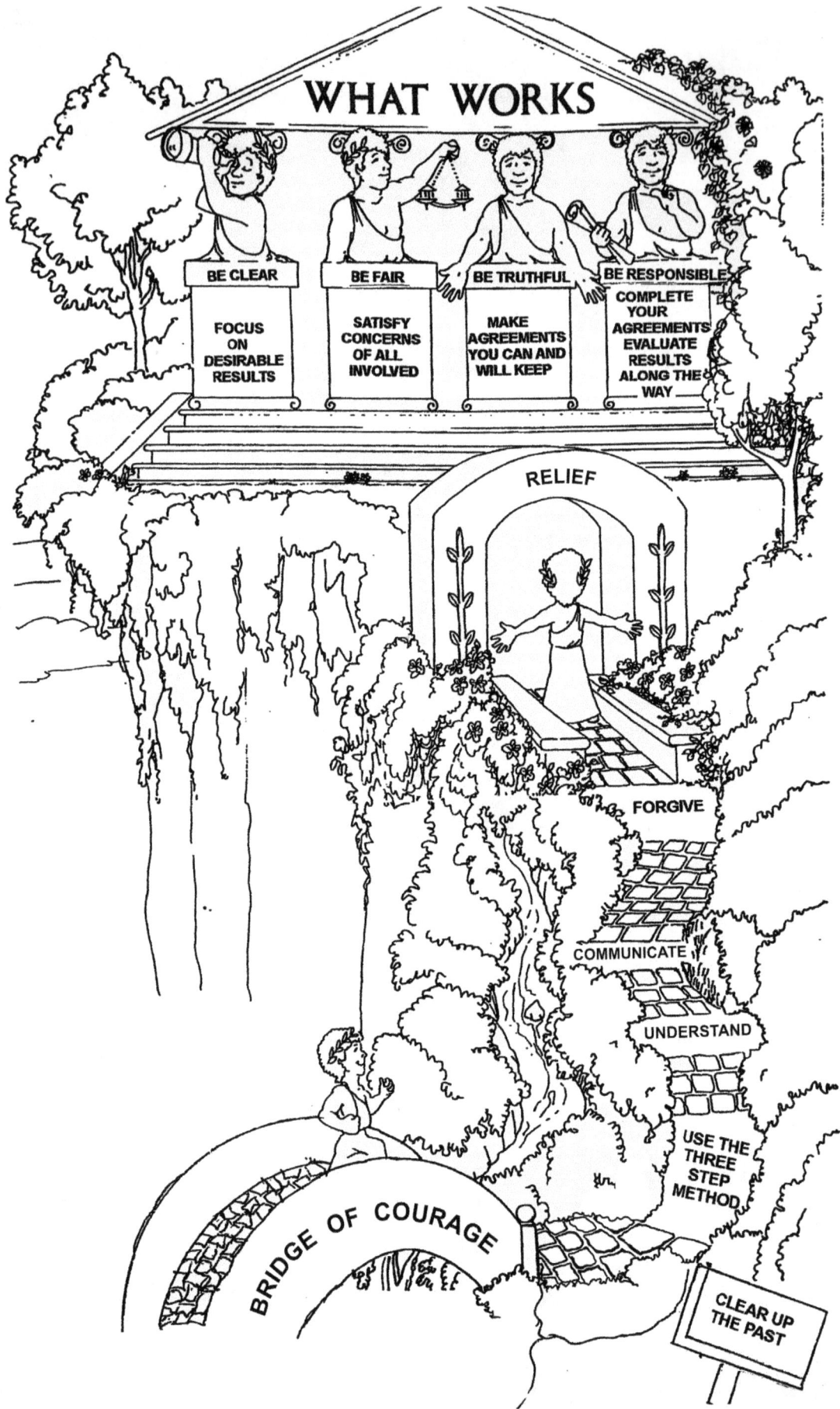

PLAYING AT WHAT WORKS

Playing At What Works has two parts - Crossing The Bridge of Courage and Playing At What Works.

Part I - Crossing The Bridge Of Courage

Crossing The Bridge of Courage is where you have the opportunity to rid yourself of any misunderstandings that may be hanging around from the past.

Part II - Playing At What Works

You are using the principles of The Game Plan; a tool that guides you toward having the life you want. Eventually these principles will become a way of managing your life with more successful outcomes.

Playing At What Works is where you want to be all the time.

CROSSING THE BRIDGE OF COURAGE
Relief

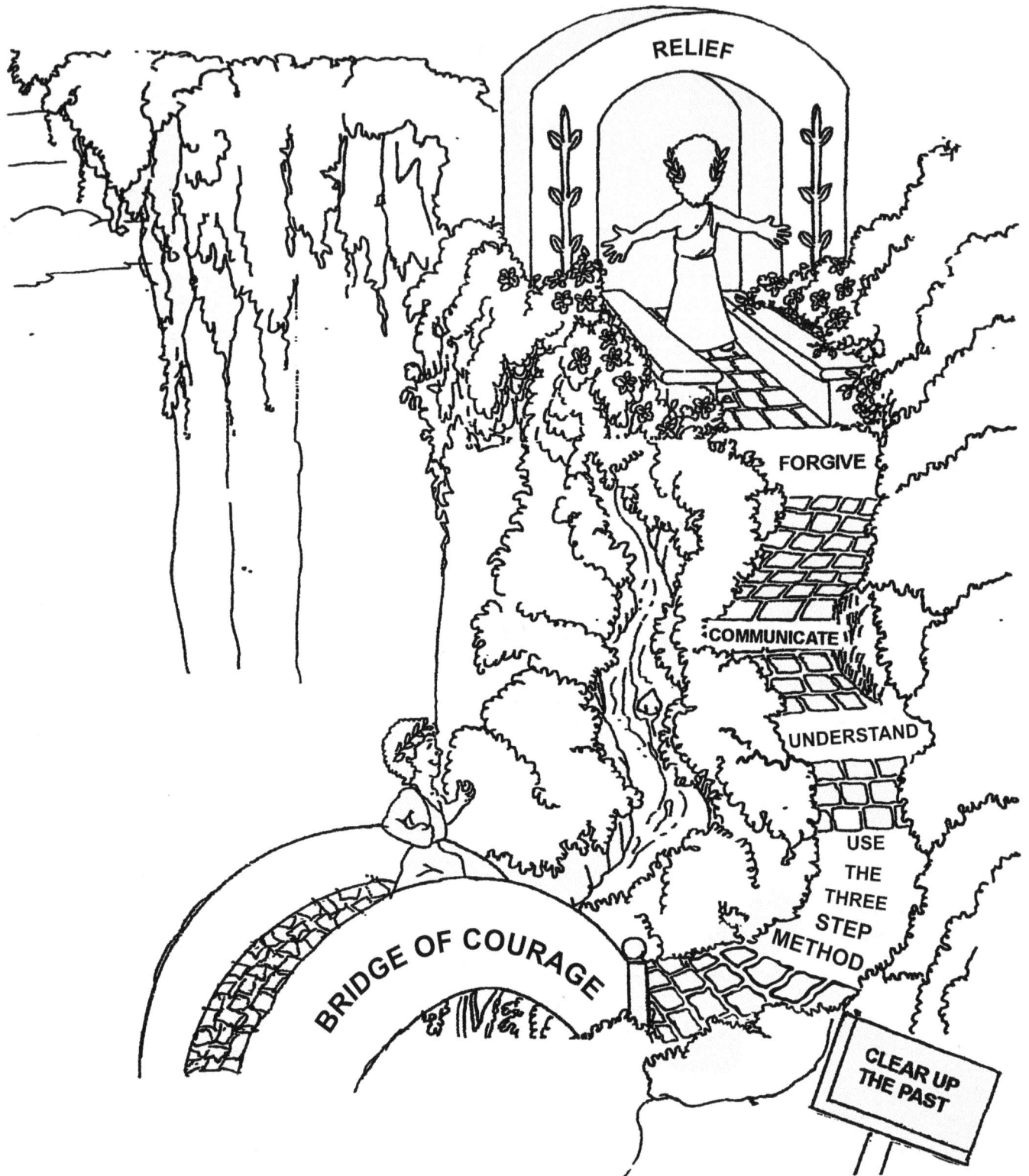

CROSSING THE BRIDGE OF COURAGE

"Acceptance of what has happened is the first step to overcoming the consequences of any misfortune."
– William James

By Crossing The Bridge of Courage and using the Three-step Method below, you will have the opportunity to clear up the past, let the situation go from your mind, and feel the resulting relief. You will be liberated from your all-consuming thoughts and concerns. You can move on.

The first step is to clear up anything that remains from the past—any problems or misunderstanding that are unresolved—so you won't have to think about them again. This is literally the process of being able to put an unsatisfactory experience out of your mind so you can focus on desirable outcomes.

When Pete and I remarried, we made a commitment to always work things out, talk things through, support each other's views and to respect our abilities and our deficiencies. Much of the time when we were angry or confused there was a cloud hanging over us. Thoughts and feelings would escalate, making the situation worse. Pete and I would say things to each other and it would be taken out of context or hurtful. Then we would react, and an argument would ensue.

However, our commitment to talk things through and get past all the rambling was a huge boost to our communication. We would say what was on our mind and, by the time we talked everything out, our dialogue and messages became clearer. We learned how to communicate with each other with more care and support. With practice, you can do this too.

It takes courage to admit you were wrong or had a part in something that didn't work out. It takes courage to stand up for what you believe in, and to face the possible rejection or adversity caused by others and the uncertainty of the future or the experience of failure. Courage gives you the strength to be committed to a worthwhile cause: you.

Believe in yourself. Stay with it. Grow and learn from your experience, including your successes and failures. Even in the face of disapproval or emotional pain, even though you are uncertain as to how it will work out, be determined to be the best you can be and clear up the past using The Three-step Method.

The Three-step Method

• **Understand what didn't work. What was my part in it?**

_____

_____

_____

• **Communicate with those involved in the situation.** Call them. Write to them. Meet them in person. Apologize when necessary. Even when others are not willing to forgive, do what it takes to clear up any issues that are unresolved. You will feel relief.

Jane's story... *A way of communication that worked for me*

There was a situation with two people that I needed to clear up. I thought about the situation so many times that I didn't want to think about them anymore. So, I wrote a letter to each person. I wrote about my feelings, and the wrongs and the rights. I told them about how their behavior affected me and how it had contributed to the loss of their friendship. I never mailed the letters. One person was no longer living. However, I took responsibility for my part in the problem. One day, I built a fire outdoors, read the letters out loud, told the people I loved them and burned the letters in the fireplace. I felt relieved and finally stopped thinking about them in a negative way. Within a week, my friend called me and we resumed our relationship as if nothing had happened. It was a surprise to me that we can clear the past in this way. Try it for yourself.

- **Forgive yourself and others for any misunderstandings.** You are both learning about yourselves. This is part of our growing process. But sometimes others are not willing to forgive and will hold on to their emotions. Just know it's time for you to move on. Forgive yourself for being involved and for doing what you did or didn't do. You need courage to be relieved and have freedom from past mistakes or misunderstandings.

Once you have cleared up the past, you will feel a lightness in your body. Your thoughts about the situation will begin to fade away. You will feel relief. Relief replaces fear, worry, doubt, guilt, confusion and all those things that were keeping your mind from functioning positively. You will have rid yourself of the burden of the past. You will have moved on to knowing that you have the choice to make your life work. You will have reached a milestone: the recognition that you are responsible for what happens in your life.

> *From Ano Ano: The Seed by Kristen Zambuka*
> *Forgive yourself for past mistakes.*
> *Let them go from your mind… the only place they ever were…*
> *hanging on like gnawing aches that spoil your present experience of life.*
> *Stop imposing the agony of remorse on yourself,*
> *and see yourself acting back then as a child… without insight*
> *… without maturity.*
> *You have grown since.*
> *The mistakes contributed to that growth.*
> *You would not act the same way now.*
> *You cannot change the past… but you can change*
> *your thoughts about it.*
> *An attitude is ours to control*
> *We are the creators.*
> *Change your thoughts and you change your world.*

Human beings are not perfect. However, when we learn from our experiences, we expand and progress with understanding and compassion for ourselves and others. We are all in this world together. We are all here to learn from our experiences and grow. This is how we contribute to our knowledge and our strengths, and it's also how we can be examples to our children, our co-workers, and our friends to encourage their development and growth. If you can do it, others can do it. If others can do it, you can do it.

It's time to move on. You are about to learn Who You Really Are. With this knowledge, you will have more control over your own body, thoughts, and emotions.

WHO ARE YOU?
Body, Mind, Emotions and Your Secret Inner Voice

WHO ARE YOU?

When we say, "me, my, and I", who is that "I"? Your body doesn't talk. It provides the organs to speak. Your mind doesn't talk. It provides the thoughts that help us make decisions and initiate actions. So then, ask yourself, "who am I?"

Many people think their physical body is who they are, but the physical body is just an organized structure with bones, flesh, and organs that work together to keep the body functioning so we can live in this world. The body includes a brain and central nervous system that sends and receives a constant stream of messages that control bodily functions, movement, thoughts, feelings, and short-term memory. The physical body is the vehicle we use to communicate with each other in our world and move us from one place to another.

The mind offers thoughts that come and go. Some thoughts are useful, others are not. Thoughts help us to learn, form concepts, make decisions, gain knowledge, develop beliefs, create experiences, and so much more. The mind operates consciously and unconsciously. We use the conscious mind to focus our attention, collect and process information, and pursue desirable outcomes. The unconscious mind is like a storage room for the information, memories, and habits we have collected along our way.

When we were hurt, angry, or upset, those feelings induced decisions, choices and behaviors that were programmed into the storage portion of the unconscious mind. When an unpleasant situation arises, we unconsciously react with unfavorable behavior based on stored memories of the past—Conditioned Behavior. The positive feelings from when we are happy and warm-hearted are also stored in the unconscious mind.

Emotions are important in providing the motivation to make decisions and direct actions that move things and ourselves along in life. Think about something you did, something that brought you happiness, joy, and good feelings. Perhaps, as a child, it was learning to play baseball, and you contributed to your team winning the game. Or maybe you wanted to play an instrument, sing or make art. These desires brought on thoughts and good feelings that caused you to learn and grow in that direction.

Be aware of your thoughts and feelings. They are what encourage you to focus on the life you want and motivate you towards the desired outcomes.

We use our five senses to see awe-inspiring sunsets, smell fragrant flowers, taste our favorite foods, hear beautiful music, and touch the people we love. What we see, hear, smell, taste, and touch help us to comprehend what is happening in our environment. Our senses create feelings and beliefs about our likes and dislikes and helps us to make judgements and decisions based on the input they provide.

When we eat something, we have thoughts and feelings about whether it tastes nice or not. We likely make a decision on whether we will eat it again. The same thing happens when we see, hear, smell, or touch something that gives us any kind of feedback. We make a decision using the information received, and that decision or choice gets stored in the unconscious part of our mind, conditioning the behavior that can affect our future. Pay attention to the information received from your senses. This will help to guide the decisions you make and the future direction and results of your life.

We all have an inner voice. It's like we are having a conversation with ourselves in our head. Sometimes it's "past conditioning" speaking to us. Some people call this the "ego". It's the voice that constantly wants to maintain a self-image or identity. It incessantly chatters about good and bad, right and wrong, and it judges and criticizes us and others in order to feel valued. When this "ego" is in charge, we live out the habits and behaviors shown on the left side of The Chart, namely Conditioned Behavior.

There is another inner voice that is much more effective in simplifying our lives and helping us create desirable outcomes. We all have it. Unfortunately, most people are not taught how to appropriately tune into their intuition.

Intuition is the ability to understand something without consciously thinking about it. It's like a voice that drops information into our head through hunches, impressions, impulses, insights, or gut feelings. You may have a question in your mind and, out of nowhere, an answer comes to you or you feel the urge to do something that provides the answer to your question. I have heard people call this a "download", an appropriate term in our modern technological world.

Intuition is a subtle guiding force that offers solutions to what we are looking for. How many times have you misplaced something and started to look for it, then a thought drops into your mind that tells you to "go here", "do this", or "look there"? Listen to your intuition. It offers an important aid to guidance and awareness, and for creating successful outcomes. Intuition is the language of our inner intelligence, our inner wisdom—our souls.

I call the physical body our Outer Being. Just as we wear our clothes on the outside of our bodies, the physical body is the outer part of who we are. It is the house in which you reside. I call who we are the Inner Being. This is the soul that drives the physical vehicle and can drive your life, if you let it.

Man is a living soul. – Paramahansa Yogananda

Physics teaches us that everything in the world is made up of matter. Matter is made of vibrating energy. The trees, our environment, the food we eat, even our bodies are composed of matter and energy. Our millions of atoms spin at the speed of light, so fast that our senses can't hear the frequency we broadcast or feel the vibration that is emitted from our bodies. We are just like AM and FM radio frequencies: our waves send out our unique frequencies. We are constantly transmitting our frequencies to the world through what we are thinking, how we are feeling, the words we use, and by the actions we take. Our body is literally transmitting our own unique vibratory frequency into the world, and the world is responding to these frequencies with our life experiences.

Everything in life is a vibration. – Albert Einstein

Let's take this theory to the next step.

There is an unseen law we live by—the Law of Attraction. The Law of Attraction is a force in our world that operates through vibrations, just like our body and the environment around us. Physics defines attraction as a force wherein two objects are influenced to move toward each other. Attraction acts as a magnet. So, what we transmit into the world through our vibrational frequency is also attracted to us. When we are transmitting thoughts and feelings of happiness and satisfaction, that vibration operates like a magnet, bringing us what makes us happy and satisfied.

We can attract unwanted experiences too. When we think negative thoughts, by criticizing people, thinking about how unhappy we are, or feeling sorry for ourselves because we are not good enough or don't have the life we want, this energy attracts more of the same. That's how the Law of Attraction operates in our lives. What we put out in our vibrations, with our thoughts and feelings, is what we attract in our life, both wanted and unwanted. This is not science fiction. This is quantum physics and metaphysics.

Inner thoughts and emotions determine the level at which one vibrates. One's vibrational rate is a frequency. This inner frequency creates a signal that is emitted outward. Once emitted, this signal begins to draw to it other things that reside on that same frequency. What is hidden within will dictate what will appear on the outside.
—The Light Shall Set You Free, by Drs. Norma Milanovich and Shirley McCune

I'm sure you've been attracted to someone because they were positive, inclusive, uplifting, or funny. Or maybe you wanted something, such as a new job, car, or home, and an opportunity appeared whereby you could attain it. Maybe you were just thinking about someone and they contacted you. These are not coincidences but examples of the Law of Attraction in action.

We see this method used all the time. A writer may have a concept in mind about what they want to write in their book or article. Then ideas begin to form that result in the finished product. This is a form of "download"—intuition that guides us to our ultimate goals. This method can be used for any goal, desire, intention, or purpose.

The Law of Attraction, written by Ester Hicks says, That which is like unto itself, is drawn. Meaning everything that you experience is attracted to you because the Law of Attraction is responding to the thoughts that you are offering. Whether you are remembering something from the past, observing something in your present, or imagining something about your future, the thought that you are focused upon in your powerful now has activated a vibration within you—and the Law of Attraction is responding to it now.

—Hicks, Ester. The Law of Attraction (Kindle Locations 711-713).
Hay House, Kindle Edition.

It's important to know how the Law of Attraction works so you can manage your thoughts, feelings, beliefs, and behavior in the present moment and use it consciously to your advantage to create the best life for yourself.

The Law of Attraction is a powerful way to create the life you want in the present. Think about the life you want. Feel what it is like to have it. Then listen to your inner voice to "download" information before you make decisions or act. This is your guide toward the desired outcome.

What is the difference between the Law of Cause and Effect discussed in Unaware of What Works and the Law of Attraction described here? The Law of Cause and Effect pertains to something you have done with your thoughts, words, and actions. It contributes to events and outcomes based on past behavior. The Law of Attraction works with your inner world, the vibration you are emitting now. Your vibration from current thoughts and feelings are attracting future experiences of a like kind.

When your words and actions are positive, the Law of Cause and Effect is working in your favor, creating events and outcomes that reflect this behavior. What you sow is what you reap! Additionally, when you focus your thoughts and feelings in a positive way, the Law of Attraction brings you the essence of the vibrations you are emitting. The good feelings you have now will attract more goodness into your life. All you need to do is to keep focused on the life you want now.

All humans are born with free will. Free will gives us the ability to make our own decisions and choices. It is our willpower that drives us to move in the direction we want. Our willpower is our strength. It demonstrates our character and perseverance. However, when we don't know or keep focused on what we want, our willpower is not used to our advantage.

One of the biggest issues we all face today is being focused and staying focused. Being focused means concentrating, being present, and being aware in all we do. Our strength lies in focusing on what we want and using our willpower to direct our choices and decisions.

There are many distractions not only in our lives but also in our world. Each of us may have a family, a job, a business, friends, special interests, televisions, computers, cell phones and social media to distract us. However, when we are focused, conscious, and putting our thoughts and feelings into our intentions, purposes, and goals, the Law of Attraction begins to respond to our frequencies and works to bring the opportunities to us. With focus and willpower, we can point our thoughts and feelings in the direction we want and attract and create desirable outcomes.

One of the favorite yoga classes I taught was the first of a series. I called it 'Body Awareness'. Attention to the body eliminates injury and teaches focus while the students were doing postures. They slowly walked around the room while I guided them to focus on parts of their body. After they completed the class, I guided them around the room to observe the release of tension from their muscles and the energy flowing through their nervous systems. They stood taller and felt more energized. It takes focus to have this awareness and to experience the many benefits of yoga.

I once read that we have 60,000 to 70,000 thoughts a day, and 90% are recycled from the day before. Wow! By thinking the same thoughts over and over, we are also cluttering our mind and possibly getting the same results at least 90% of the time. Is this using our will productively? Is this being focused?

As you know, it is essential to quiet our mental chatter. This helps to clear our mind, so guidance in the form of our intuition can be heard. When we develop the skills to focus on something specific, we can use our good feelings and willpower to energize our intentions and visions for our future. We can emit these vibrations, as if asking for it, and watch the opportunities come to us.

I think we humans complicate our lives too much. We spend too much time in the past thinking about mistakes, feeling sorry for ourselves, and being angry or critical of others. All this chatter takes a toll on our lives and keeps us busy in the past. These are not uplifting thoughts. This is not being focused on what you want. You are not creating the future you want. The past is there for you to learn from. The present is here for you to shape your life as you want it to be, and to enjoy.

I'm sure you've heard expressions like, "the past is gone", "the future is not here", "the present is all that exists", and, "your power is in the present moment". The way to have the life you desire is to focus on what you want and live in the present moment more and more each day. This is using your focus and willpower appropriately. When you are present, you are awake: you are conscious, you are aware, and you are "Being".

In order to experience "Being", you must go through a process that takes patience because you will be developing a new skill and becoming who you want to be: someone who is consciously creating a life that is desirable and brings happiness. We're here to learn and grow from our successes and failures, and this is a continual process.

If you are unhappy about the way things are turning out in your life, it's time to wake up to reality: you *do* have control over your life. You are responsible for your life being what it is, and you are responsible for your life being what you want it to be.

Continually focus your thoughts your feelings on your desires and the happiness you want.

Focus on what you want and enjoy the journey that goes along with having it. This is not selfish. As you become a better person, you'll have more opportunities to show others what can be by example.

We are equipped with all we need to achieve wellbeing and a balanced life. Your thoughts and feelings have power. They can cause negative or positive actions and outcomes. Focus on the joy of having a productive and healthy life. Be Present. Listen to your Inner Being, or intuition, and follow your heart. This will send out vibrations to attract happiness, satisfaction, and wellbeing.

We always want more in life because life provides us with the knowledge to grow and become better, more satisfied people. Growing and becoming better people is our mission in life. The Awareness Game principles will show you how to be more focused aware, and in charge by using your willpower to get you the life you want. All you need to do to get there is know what you want, which the Game will help you with. Keep your focus on the desired outcome, and apply the principles of The Game Plan. All this is coming up next.

WHAT WORKS
The Game of Offer and Accept

WHAT WORKS

BE CLEAR

FOCUS
ON
DESIRABLE
RESULTS

BE FAIR

SATISFY
CONCERNS
OF ALL
INVOLVED

BE TRUTHFUL

MAKE
AGREEMENTS
YOU CAN AND
WILL KEEP

BE RESPONSIBLE

COMPLETE
YOUR
AGREEMENTS
EVALUATE
RESULTS
ALONG THE
WAY

WHAT WORKS

'What Works' will teach you how to be successful in your endeavors, have supportive relationships, experience satisfaction and happiness, and feel secure about your future outcomes. What Works provides The Game Plan—a method that helps you work towards where you want to be in life.

Many people say they don't know what they want or where they want to be in life, but everyone knows what they don't want. For instance, no one wants results below expectations, uncomfortable feelings or negative outcomes. However, even this discomfort offers an opportunity for change and improvement. So, when unsatisfactory situations come up, ask yourself, "What would I rather have or do instead of this?"

To get what you want you must know what you want. Luckily, you can foster thoughts and ideas about what you want simply by using your natural abilities and creativity to imagine or visualize your desired outcome.

Creativity means envisioning what can be and bringing it into existence. There is no mystery or secret to being creative. Use your imagination to spark ideas and the motivation to help you gain more clarity on what you want in order to make things better in your life.

Some people say they don't see images in their mind. They don't visualize. This might be you. That's ok! You might have thoughts, inspiration, motivation, feelings, or intuition that drives you instead. These are also natural creative powers that provide momentum and can begin the process of directing your future towards what you want. Pay attention to what motivates you and makes you feel good. This is the fuel needed to achieve successful outcomes.

Some people tend to think of creativity as the exclusive domain of a painter, writer, composer, inventor, etc. However, everyone is creative and resourceful. Everyone is designing their life, all the time. You create the way you look with the clothes you wear and the styles you adopt. You create the way you feel about yourself and others. You create what you are going to do through the choices you make, and you use these natural creative abilities to plan your future. Use your mind appropriately: fill it with uplifting thoughts and feelings. This will begin the process of attracting the life you want.

We all have an imagination that can be used to form ideas. Simply by using your ability to dream, fantasize, visualize, and think, you can start the process of changing something in your life. When you imagine something in your mind, you start having more thoughts about it. These thoughts make it possible to come up with more ideas that help you make appropriate decisions that lead toward achieving the desired outcome.

Think about something you wanted. Let's say it was a new car. Once you had the idea about it you came up with more thoughts, like what kind of car it would be and the color and features you wanted in that car. Maybe you searched the internet or went out to see several different makes and models to determine what was available and best for you. These thoughts helped give you clarity on what car you ultimately decided to buy. This goes for anything. Using your natural abilities this way will create what you want.

Our greatest discoveries have come from people just like us who were able to imagine a result others could not. The lightbulb was real for Edison, even though he failed over a thousand times before he brought it into existence. That's just one example. The way we live today compared to the way people lived 100 years ago is the result of the creativity and courage of each individual who thought of a better way of doing something and then did it. They believed in what they were doing. They created a better life with their thoughts, ideas, and creative ability—not only for themselves but for others too.

After practicing the principles of The Game Plan for a while, you will begin to use them as a new way of thinking and life management. You will live your life naturally, with more clarity, focus and understanding for yourself and others. When you have clarity on an intention or objective, and understand how to achieve it, you can make decisions that are right for you.

What you do does not define who you are.
What you learn about yourself and
What you become is what is important.
Author Unknown

So, to begin the process of learning what you want, we will start by focusing on a few areas of your life. You will be filling out an inventory list of Where You Want to Be. Then, you will use the principles in The Game Plan to direct you towards that desire.

WHERE YOU WANT TO BE

Experience Wellbeing and a Balanced Life with:
Success • Support • Satisfaction • Security

WHERE
YOU WANT TO BE

Successful businesses have a mission statement. It is a declaration of the product or service they want to provide their customers, and of how the company will ensure success in delivering it. A mission statement is an intention: an announcement of where you want to be. The Awareness Game has a mission statement, a purpose to work toward, and a direction to move in.

The Awareness Game is an easy, four step approach for
changing, improving, and creating the life you want.

People can have mission statements, too. Think about what you want in your life. What is your intention or purpose for being here? What do you want to accomplish while you are here? What do you want to change, improve, and create in your life?

In my thirties, I never thought about where I wanted to be or about having a personal mission to direct my life. I didn't have time to look at myself and discover what I wanted or where I wanted to be in my life. Or so I told myself.

When my children had moved out and Pete and I married, I started questioning what my purpose in life was. What interests do I have? What direction do I want to go? What areas of my life do I want to develop and make better?

I started writing out my mission statement, my purpose, my declaration of Where I Want to Be. It took a while before my statement was written in a way that made sense. I wanted to be a better person than I was. I wanted to develop some characteristics and qualities, such as compassion for myself and others so I could expand my understanding as opposed to my criticism. I wanted to be happy.

Then, thoughts and ideas began to come to me. The "how to do it" began to unfold and Pete had a method, The Game Plan, that provided the direction for my mission.

Your purpose or mission statement is an evolutionary process that spans your life. It's not a goal you achieve before you move on to another goal. You will always be working toward your purpose—that's the point of a mission statement. It provides you with the direction you want to go in life.

So, what's your mission in life? You can begin by using the inventory list below to direct you toward the answer. Then, use The Game Plan to plot your path.

Here's an example of a mission statement I wrote for myself regarding physical health:

I have a healthy, strong, toned physical body using appropriate exercise and a high-nutrient diet that supports my ideal body size and weight.

You can see this statement is an affirmation, written in the present as though I already experience it. It's not a goal but a process of becoming and maintaining my physical health throughout my life.

Below, you will find an inventory list of Where You Want to Be. In the first part of this Guidebook, you wrote down some ideas for certain areas of your life regarding things you want to change, improve, and create in your life. Go back to the section, 'What's It All About?' on page 15. You will begin to define those ideas while answering the questions below.

Think about the answers to each question. Visualize or imagine the end result. In my example above, the result I want to achieve and maintain is a healthy, strong, flexible physical body. I am using exercise, diet and any other ideas that may "download" later to work on this result. Then, I designed how I was going to carry out my intention using The Game Plan.

As your ideas begin to "download", you can define your statement below more clearly. Answer in a sentence or two:

- *What is the result I want?*
- *What am I doing to carry out my intention?*
- *What would it look like and be like?*

In terms of success and control of over my life:

_____

_____

_____

_____

In describing supportive relationships with others:

_____

_____

_____

_____

In terms of my personal satisfaction and contentment:

_____

_____

_____

_____

In describing a sense of security and certainty about my future:

_____

_____

_____

_____

You have identified some of the areas of Where You Want to Be. Keep refining your intentions in these areas and add other areas you want to change, improve, or create. Thoughts about these intentions will come appearing in your mind, allowing you to explore the many options available to you. Pay attention to your thoughts and how you are feeling about the ideas coming into your mind. They are providing you with information about what to do. Be attentive to the decisions you are making.

Use the principles of The Game Plan on each of your answers and the other intentions that you may develop. The principles are a guide to your future. The more you use The Game Plan, the faster you will learn to live naturally and create the life you want.

THE GAME PLAN

Clarity • Understanding • Agreement • Success

The Game Plan is a method that guides you to Where You Want To Be. It has four principles. Each principle has questions that direct you to think, envision, and focus on your mission in life. It will provide a step by step process to accomplish it. Here are the principles:

- **Be Clear** - To have clarity you must know what you want. You identified much of this when you answered the questions in 'Where You Want to Be'.

- **Be Fair** - To gain understanding you must be fair by addressing your concerns and the concerns of those involved.

- **Be Truthful** - To reach agreement you must be truthful about what you can and will do.

- **Be Responsible** - To achieve the results you want you must be responsible, do your part and evaluate your results along the way.

Now, if you dismiss these concepts as being too simple, too idealistic or too naive, you must listen to the often-told story of the Zen master and the disciple.

The disciple went to the Zen master and asked, "Tell me, master, what is the secret to the meaning of life?" The master replied, "Work when you work, eat when you eat, rest when you rest." The disciple said, "But master, that is so simple." "Yes," replied the master, "but so few people seem to be able to do it."

The principles of The Game Plan may sound simple, but it takes practice to create new habits of thinking. It takes focusing on the outcome to realize the results you want. It takes awareness of the feelings that may be keeping you from moving toward the successes you want. As Deepak Chopra says, "The secret to happiness is to be present." Being Present is staying focused on what is happening now. Focus means making yourself a priority and paying attention to your daily life.

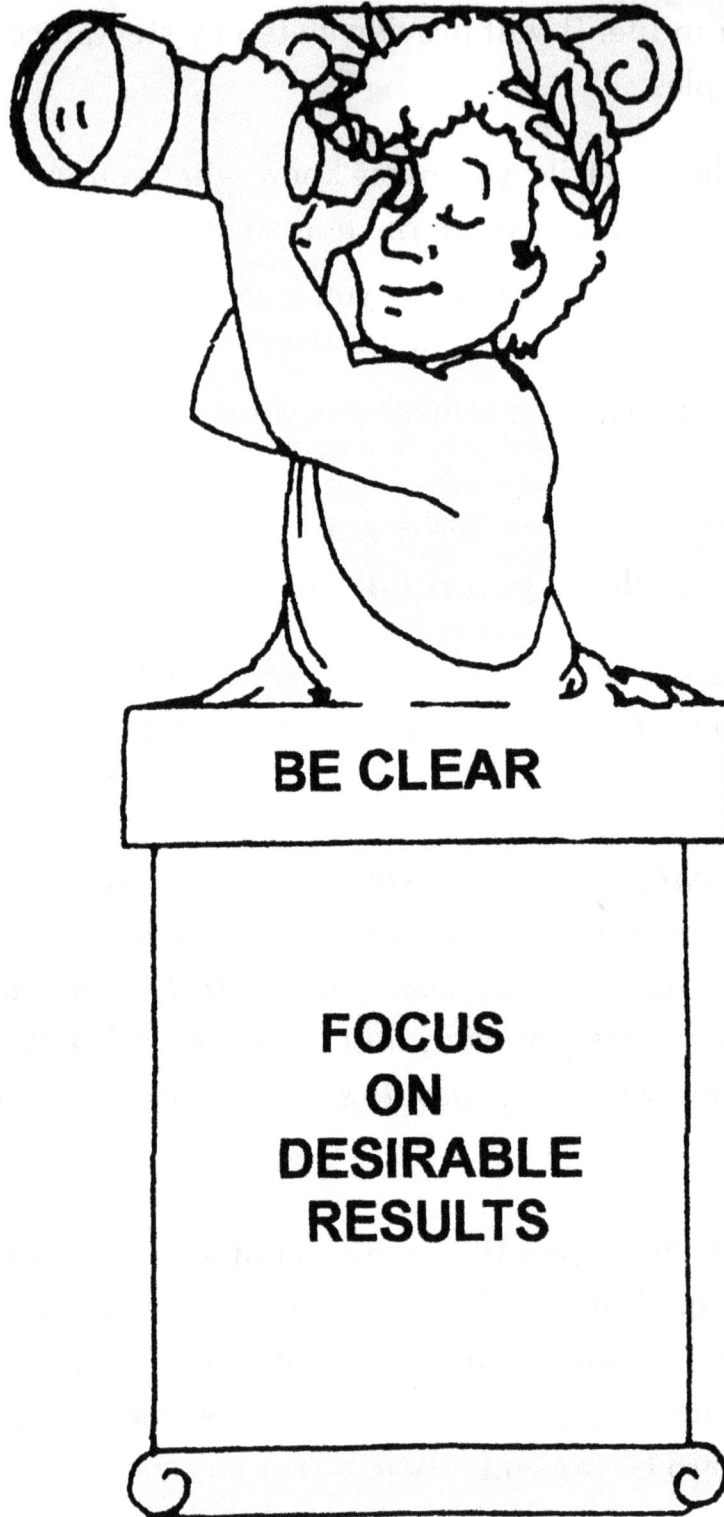

BE CLEAR

FOCUS
ON
DESIRABLE
RESULTS

PRINCIPLE # 1 - BE CLEAR
FOCUS ON DESIRABLE RESULTS

Life is about taking the time to develop into the person you want to be. It is about finding the passion and drive to build qualities and internal strengths, and knowing what you want and going after it by focusing on it.

The billionaire was very clear about what he wanted. He could come up with an idea and follow it through to completion. He was successful in accomplishing the results he wanted in business because he was always focused on the outcome.

Pete's Story: *It's All About Focus*

I used to sit on my deck overlooking Lake Tahoe, watching the clouds. I would pick out a cloud and focus on it with the intention of vaporizing it, and it always worked. You can do this too. All you need is to focus your attention for a minute or two, with your intention to make the cloud disappear, and the cloud will vanish. When you focus on the result you want with intention and feeling, you can make it happen.

Every day is a potential work of art. Your life, relationships, business, projects, thoughts, feelings and experiences are your canvas, your clay. It is your choice. Keep focusing on your intentions and desirable outcomes. The momentum created by this focus will help you get there.

You are about to embark on a journey that will shape your life as you want it to be. Take one of your intentions from the list of Where You Want to Be. Start writing out your answers below:

• **What do I want?** What is the intention, desire, or outcome? Write it out as if you already have it.

_____

_____

_____

_____

_____

• **How does this benefit me?**

_____

_____

_____

_____

_____

• **How does this benefit others?**

_____

_____

_____

_____

_____

As you consider your answers, more thoughts and information will come to you. Moreover, start to pay attention to what you are thinking and the experiences you are having throughout your day. They could contain indications of the next step to take toward what you want.

Sometimes your motivation behind the objective may lessen, or the objective may cease to be desirable. Perhaps the time is not right. Have the courage to let it go and focus on another objective, intention, or desire.

BE FAIR

**SATISFY
CONCERNS
OF ALL
INVOLVED**

PRINCIPLE #2 - BE FAIR
SATISFY THE CONCERNS OF ALL INVOLVED

The second step to having what you want is to obtain an understanding of what and who is involved so you can make appropriate decisions.

In my example about using exercise to maintain my physical health, I decided what kind of exercise I liked, as well as where and how I was going to do them. I had questions and concerns to answer before I decided to do them. Satisfying my concerns provided understanding. Understanding created agreement with the method I would use for my intention.

Others may also be involved in this decision. To be fair and gain support from others, you must satisfy their concerns. Be open, understand their questions, and communicate your ideas clearly to them while providing room for all involved to brainstorm ideas that could make an outcome even better. When you or others have a question or an objection, you should come to an understanding by answering any concerns.

You have been around children that are constantly asking questions. "What is that for?", "how does that work?", and on and on. Your responses to these questions help the child understand the world better. The same happens when you are planning a trip with someone. There are questions and concerns about where to go, what to see, and how to travel. Satisfying concerns is the way to be fair with everyone that is involved.

Let's examine the art of expressing positive energy and power and how it can change your outcome. We'll start with an idea called The Chicken Soup Theory.

The Chicken Soup Theory is based on the old notion that when a child got sick and Mom made some chicken soup, the child got well. It has long been suspected that the love and care that went into making the soup for the child had a lot more to do with the child getting well than the soup itself.

This is not an unusual concept. Most of us have experienced the power of love. This power is very real. It exists and we are affected by it. We are drawn to people who make us feel good, who care about us, and who encourage us. One of the greatest feelings you can experience—being in love—is the result of two people giving and receiving the power of love. Thinking good thoughts and having good feelings about someone makes them feel good in the same way that the child who eats the chicken soup gets well.

This power works in many ways. We see it in the spirit of Christmas. The home field advantage. The support we feel from teamwork. The comfortable feeling that comes from being with certain people. The excitement and dedication that one brings to a worthwhile challenge.

The positive energy we generate is the healing part of the chicken soup. Caring about someone and wanting to empower others is a good way to share this positive power. When we empower others, we are empowered ourselves.

We are all "chicken soup factories" that, with others, create alignment, synergy and support. This is what makes relationships work. This power—the good feelings we give and receive—is what we use to help us achieve a balanced life of success, support, satisfaction, and security. Satisfying concerns and gaining understanding with those involved creates supportive relationships.

Supportive relationships are an important factor because we are social beings and want relationships with others. When you treat people the way you would like to be treated, and when you are fair to them, you receive their support and participation. Everyone benefits.

Answer the questions below; both when it applies to you and others are involved:

- **From whom do I need agreement?** *Who else is involved in obtaining what I want?*

Just you?   Who are the others?

_____   _____

_____   _____

_____   _____

_____   _____

- **What do I or others need to know?** *What skills and talents are needed?*

_____

_____

_____

- **Where will I get this knowledge or information?**

_____

_____

_____

Cooperation, teamwork, synergy and alignment occur when there is a common understanding of the objective. When others have the same clear picture of what is essential to achieve an objective, they will have clarity and understanding and become co-creators of the desired outcome.

PRINCIPLE #3 - BE TRUTHFUL
MAKE AGREEMENTS YOU CAN AND WILL KEEP

The third step to having what you want is to agree on how it will be done. What is going to happen?

The secret to developing a strategy that will work is to be truthful about what you can and will do. When you make an agreement to do something, be certain that you can say to yourself, "I am willing and able to do it because I want to".

Being truthful with others is an essential ingredient in establishing reliability, maintaining trust, and experiencing the satisfaction from a job well done. When people cannot trust each other, they cannot be free from the worry or fear that can lead to disagreement. Justifying your position or blaming others for things not working out is the behavior shown on the left side of The Chart—Unaware of What Works.

Recognize that an intention can be carried out when you and those involved are each willing and able to do their part. If it turns out that you can't complete your agreement, communicate what isn't working, and make a new agreement that will work for you and those involved. This is being truthful and keeps you moving toward the desired outcome.

Pete's Story – Win Your Wings of Gold. Become an Aviation Cadet.

That was the advertisement. I believed it, and there I was. This was my first day on the base, on my way toward winning the coveted Wings of Gold, July 1941.

And, where was I? Standing in the middle of a room in the barracks that contained twenty urinals and twelve toilets. Standing there with a bucket of cleaning fluid in one hand, and a rag in the other. Mad as can be. This is not what Aviators do. This is not what Stanford graduates do. It is certainly not the type of thing that I do. As I pondered the irrevocable blunder I had made, another aviation cadet walked in with a bucket and rag, took one look at me, and said, "Well, let's get the job done."

It was the start of a lasting friendship. His name was John. A graduate of Cal and an outstanding athlete, he had resigned his commission as an Ensign to go through the ranks again to become a pilot.

The first time we were given liberty, I invited him to spend the weekend at my parents' apartment in San Francisco. We went to a local bar and had drinks. There were two very attractive young ladies sitting together at a table. John said, "Why don't you go over and ask if we could join them."

I replied, "This is our first night out. Let's just have a few drinks and see what develops. After all, we have the whole weekend."

John said, "I'd go ask them, but I don't have the guts."

I've never forgotten that seemingly unimportant incident. It made me realize how often in my life I had been dishonest with myself and others because I hadn't wanted to be rejected. I saw how many times I had been dishonest about what I was willing and able to do just so someone would accept or appreciate me.

Be aware of the times when you find yourself lying because you are afraid of what might happen.

Formulate your plan by answering the questions below:

- **How will it be done?** *Think about the outcome you want. What steps or actions are required to achieve your desired result? You might not know all the steps yet but, as you focus on the outcome you want and begin to carry out your plan, more ideas will come to you.*

_____

_____

_____

- **Who will do it?** *Who will take responsibility for what needs to be done? Am I willing and able to participate? Are others willing and able to participate?*

You   Others

_____   _____

_____   _____

_____   _____

- **When will it be done?** *Is there a time factor involved? Not all results will have a completion date. For instance, developing a skill like golf or painting or a quality like kindness or compassion could likely be an ongoing process.*

_____

_____

_____

- **When others are involved, is there an established method for feedback? How will feedback be conveyed?** *If something isn't working out, communicate and create a new plan that enables you and others to accomplish the objective.*

_____

_____

_____

To achieve satisfaction in your life, be truthful about what you can and will carry out. You may be willing to do something but not able or you may be able to do something but not willing. When you and others are willing and able, agreements can be reached and results will be accomplished.

When it is obvious that the goals cannot be reached,
don't adjust the goals, adjust the action steps. —Confucius

BE RESPONSIBLE

COMPLETE
YOUR
AGREEMENTS
EVALUATE
RESULTS
ALONG THE
WAY

PRINCIPLE #4 - BE RESPONSIBLE
COMPLETE YOUR AGREEMENTS AND EVALUATE THE RESULTS ALONG THE WAY

The last step toward having what you want is to follow the plan you have agreed upon and evaluate your results along the way. Results are created when everyone is doing their part. That's being responsible! Knowing you can be counted on and that you can count on others eliminates doubt and uncertainty. Having certainty will keep your mind focused on accomplishing the desired result.

Pete's Story: A Story About Uncertainty

Up until now, the most meaningful experience of my whole life was when I was flying my single-engine airplane and the engine quit. It was caused by the connecting rod between the piston and the crankshaft breaking, causing a loss of power and a loud clanking noise.

I was about 20 miles from San Jose, a California airport. I tuned in the emergency radio frequency and broadcast a "mayday", the international call for help. The San Jose tower answered and cleared me for an emergency landing. When I was over the city, three miles from the runway and at a low altitude, the connecting rod jammed the crankshaft and, with a puff of smoke and flame, the engine stopped.

I looked for a place to land. The only open space I saw was a small field bordered by trees. I felt I could land in the field and avoid any populated areas, but it was probable that I would hit the trees before the plane came to a stop.

How did I feel about this? I had been a Marine dive-bomber pilot in World War II and had been afraid many times that I might die but I'd never been sure of it. This time turned out to be different. This time, over San Jose, I was certain. At that moment, I knew I was going to die and that's when the experience became so full of meaning. A voice, out of my head, said, loud and clear, "Well, it looks as if you'll get to find out if there is anything beyond this life, after all."

Anticlimactically, almost immediately, I saw a freeway that was under construction out of the corner of my eye. It was unoccupied, and so I was able to make a safe landing on it. When the plane rolled to a stop, the same voice said, "Boy, am I glad to be alive."

I was totally surprised by the experience. I'd had no idea how I would actually feel if I knew I was going to die. I did not know that I wouldn't be afraid but that is what happened. As time passed, it has become clearer and clearer to me that uncertainty is what causes fear. The fear of what might happen.

Learning to navigate uncertainty without fear is part of the process of seeing things clearly. Uncertainty is part of a learning experience which leads to knowledge. Knowledge gives you more certainty and awareness of the future.

Certainty keeps your mind focused on the outcome because you aren't distracted by worrying about what might happen. Your thoughts are focused on accomplishing your intention—your objective.

When things are not turning out as you had hoped, evaluate the situation to see what worked and what didn't. Come up with new ideas, look at your choices and make decisions that enable you to accomplish your objective.

Evaluate the results along the way by answering the questions below:

• **What is working?** *What results are satisfying?*

_____

_____

_____

• **What isn't working?**

What results are below expectation?   What needs improvement?

_____   _____

_____   _____

_____   _____

• **What could work better?**

What can I change?   What is my objective now?

_____   _____

_____   _____

_____   _____

If you have a new objective now, look at steps 1, 2, and 3 above to see if you need to add more clarity to What Could Work Better.

When there is clarity on an objective and understanding about what is involved in achieving it, decisions can be made, agreements reached, and results accomplished. —The Awareness Game

You have now learned the principles of The Game Plan: Playing at What Works. The answers to these questions will keep you focused and provide the momentum to move you toward your desired intention or outcome. Use The Game Plan to your advantage. What you think, feel, and do will attract what you experience, both the wanted and unwanted. Create the life you want. Use the principles of The Game Plan to help make that happen.

THE GAME PLAN SUMMARY

Where Do You Want to Be in your life? When determining what you want, making a decision, agreeing to do something, or planning a project or personal goal, use the steps below to be clear about what you want and how you will accomplish it. Use The Game Plan until you have learned to follow these steps automatically, so your life experiences are in *your* control instead of the rest of the world's.

Step 1 - BE CLEAR

Focus on desirable results.

What do I want?

How does this benefit me?

How does this benefit others?

Step 2 - BE FAIR

Satisfy the concerns of all involved.

From whom do I need agreement?

What do I or others need to know?

Where will I get this knowledge or information?

Step 3 - BE TRUTHFUL

Make agreements you can and will keep.

How will it be done?

Who will do it?

When will it be done?

Is there an established method for feedback?

Step 4 - BE RESPONSIBLE

Complete your agreements and evaluate results along the way.

What is working?

What isn't working?

What could work better?

Use steps 1, 2 and 3 on What Could Work Better

When there is clarity on an objective and understanding about what is involved in achieving it, decisions can be made, agreements reached, and results accomplished. —The Awareness Game

WHERE DID YOU PLAY TODAY?

You now know Where You Want to Be. You looked at the past and discovered old beliefs and motives that no longer work for you. You examined the present by recognizing what you want to change, improve, and create in your life. You began to create your future using the four principles of The Game Plan. Now it is time for you to do your part.

Playing The Awareness Game takes practice. As you start to play, remember that no golfer, skier, tennis player, or baseball player did very well the first time they tried the sport. With practice, however, they learned how to be good at their sport and to enjoy it. Similarly, you will develop your skills. As you become more accomplished at playing The Awareness Game, the times when you are not playing at What Works will become less frequent and shorter in duration.

To have an enjoyable and successful life, use The Awareness Game until it becomes a way of living with integrity, compassion, honesty, and responsibility. Be appreciative of the progress you are undergoing along the way. Even learning experiences and failures from past decisions will help your personal development and growth. Disparity, contradiction, and conflict are all ways we learn about what we don't want. When you know what you don't want, you are given the opportunity to decide what you do want.

Be in touch with your feelings, because they are the indications of whether to move forward or not. Your feelings, good and the bad, will point you in that direction. Understanding, compassion, and caring for yourself and others will help you move in that direction, because the vibration you are emitting attracts the outcomes through your thoughts and feelings. Use them positively to create the best possible outcomes in your life. This is how you use the Law of Attraction to your advantage.

I believe that everyone has a desire to be their best. Maintaining your health, and using your thoughts and emotions appropriately is the ultimate gift one can give themself. I encourage you to be attentive to what you are thinking and how you are feeling about what is happening to you. Your future depends on it.

HOW TO PLAY THE AWARENESS GAME

- Read The Guidebook over until you understand how to change, improve and create what you want.

- If you haven't already done so, fill out your Personal Inventory list of Where You Want to Be. Continue to add to your list.

- Use The Game Plan to achieve what is on your Personal Inventory list.

- Look at The Chart*, on the cover, every day.

- When something is not working out, follow the path through The Chart to identify where you are playing in this situation. Then, you can use the appropriate solutions along the way to move up the path to Playing At What Works.

- Continue to use the principles of The Game Plan to help you become the master of your own life, creating and having desirable outcomes. The principles will become a new way of managing your life.

Remember you are a player in life and you are the one that has control of your life. Treat yourself and others with respect and kindness. Use your willpower appropriately to create a life that works for you and provide support to others' on their pathways to success. The more you learn about what does and doesn't work for you, the better you become. Becoming the best you can be is your ultimate purpose in life.

We all want to experience wellbeing and a balanced life with Success as the outcome, Support from others, Satisfaction from a job well done, and Security in our future endeavors. Look at your daily life. Is it contributing to what you want? Continue to use The Awareness Game to help you direct your life to where you want it to be.

Much love to you throughout your journey.
Pete and Jane

* A larger size, 16" x 20", of The Awareness Game Chart is available to frame or hang on your wall. Contact - playtheawarenessgame@gmail.com.

ABOUT JANE WANGER FALKE

At 38, Jane attended a six-week live-in experience at the Burklyn Business School. It taught entrepreneurship as well as a holistic approach to wellbeing. Pete Wanger was one of the owners and teachers. He became her mentor and then her husband.

Their relationship was based on the principles and methods that developed into *The Awareness Game*. Using these principles, Jane discovered her interests in yoga and meditation, got certified as a yoga teacher, and taught it for 25 years. She developed a DVD called 'Inner Yoga,' and published her first book, *The Meditation Course; a Journey of Self-Discovery*.

When Pete passed away, his only regret was that he never brought *The Awareness Game* to the world to help people to create a better, more conscious life for themselves. In Jane's last words to him, she promised that she would.

Jane found another passion in nutrition. She acquired a Master's degree in Holistic Nutrition and started a business, The Nutritionist Naturally. She published a second book, *Eat Healthy Be Healthy at Any Age*.

Retired now, Jane remarried but she never forgot Pete's dream and her promise to him. The principles outlined in *The Awareness Game* will change your life for the better.

www.ingramcontent.com/pod-product-compliance
Lightning Source LLC
Chambersburg PA
CBHW062103090426
42741CB00015B/3317